Your Super,
Natural
Mind

Your Super, Natural Mind

by
Sandra McNeil

A Nicholson Press Book

ANGUS & ROBERTSON PUBLISHERS

Acknowledgements

I would like to thank Patrick Crean and Allan Stormont of The Nicholson Press. Other thanks go to Dr. James Julian, M.D., Dr. Robert Ruder, Mildred Finnel, Helen Giuliani, Quindina Giuliani, and Christopher Harris.

ANGUS & ROBERTSON PUBLISHERS
London. Sydney. Melbourne. Singapore. Manila

First published by Angus & Robertson Publishers, 1981

ISBN Hardcover 0 207 95983 8
       Softcover 0 207 95984 6

The Nicholson Press
9 Sultan Street
Toronto, Ontario M5S 1L6

Printed in The United States of America

Dedicated To

My Beloved Husband
Terrence R. Clifton

Table of Contents

Foreword

According to legend, when the Creator of all things had finished crowning his work with the creation of the human being, He fell upon a dilemma....

Where should He hide the key to the mystery of this human creature, so that it would remain safe until needed? For if ever this code were discovered before man was ready for it, it might be used for negative or destructive ends. Therefore, it must be carefully hidden.

The Creator mused: "If I place it at the top of the highest mountain, man will eventually learn to scale the mountain.

"If I bury it in the deepest caverns below the earth, man will eventually learn to dig into the earth.

"And if I sink it in the deepest part of the ocean, man in his constant searching is certain to learn to dive down there too.

"Where then shall I place the code to this human mystery I have created? Where shall I place the owner's manual? So that man will only find it when he is sufficiently far advanced to be able to use it with proper respect and understanding. Where is the last place a human being would look for it?

"The only place completely secure from premature discovery, where only diligence, dedication and perseverance can locate it, *is deep within the self.*"

From this remote beginning, man has since evolved through various stages — including dark eras of superstitious fear of the unknown, periods of religious tyranny, and times of complete devotion to science and technology — all in an unending effort to improve and expand the experience of life and understanding of our universe.

Now, with the exploration of outer space, the realization is beginning to dawn that answers to our universe are not always just beyond the next outer limit. Instead, human beings are beginning to stop and listen to themselves: within the self.

Astronauts are unique because they have been in space and have been able to look back at our planet. They have a viewpoint of life that permeates their post-space existences. They are sought after, honored, offered choice positions in the environmental, political, religious and economic spheres. We feel they have an edge on the rest of us because they have been where we have not been and cannot go.

"Intronauts" is a word I've coined at this time to describe those individuals fortunate and brave enough to explore the inner limits of the Mind — the ultimate last frontier!

Anyone who has admired, envied or even been interested in the feats of extraterrestrial travel and phenomena will jump at the opportunity to have experiences at least equal to and possibly superior to those of historic adventurers including the recent astronauts.

Sandra NcNeil has enlarged the body owner's manual from the state of simple flyers on single aspects such as meditation, accupressure, massage, etc., to the expanded working text within the covers of this book. It can revolutionize, for those who apply it, the very nature of your perceptions and experience and, quite possibly, even your very existence.

Thank you, Sandra. Happy voyage, reader!

James J. Julian, M.D.
Julian Holistic Medical Center
Hollywood, California

Introduction

This book has been in me for some time. Throughout my life, I have become increasingly aware that there exists between us all an "inner communication" or psychic connection. This level of communication, silent and deep, transcends all pretense and doubletalk that occur in what we call "real life" — our daily dealings with one another.

The amazing thing is that most people are not aware that such communication exists. Most people, raised to be rational, "level-headed" and civilized, have by-passed the most powerful level of communication there is, the gut level of communication. This powerful level of communication is reachable only through the psychic level of mind — a level of mind we all possess.

My own psychic abilities were developed due to a nomadic childhood as a "railroad kid." My dad worked for the Santa Fe Railroad, and I was raised on a diet of scrambling among new and strange towns, schools, teachers and neighbors (to say nothing of new school policies to assimilate, neighborhood bullies to survive and "in-groups" to please). In my seventh-grade year, I changed schools eight times. I remember the day I arrived in Topeka, Kansas. Straight from an Indian reservation school in Arizona, and proudly turned out in a hooped squaw skirt and rawhide Indian boots, I was welcomed with snickers and whispers at school. Thirty heads turned at once, causing an "air" of shock. I knew that they thought I was in costume. To make things worse, I could "feel" them knowing I wanted to hide under a rock.

In the mad scramble to adjust, fit in and be a part of so many peculiar and varying rules and styles, I developed an *inner sense* that enabled me to know on-the-spot, and just as important, to know ahead of time, what the new kids in the next town were like, what the styles were, what the teachers were like (an essential for survival), and an inner sense of what people in general were feeling.

With practice, I could not only get intense feelings from others, but could actually see "inside my head" viewmaster-like slides that could show me a fellow student or teacher in some scene or other from his life. Sometimes the scene would be from his past, at other times of the future.

Bedtime was spent lying on my bunkbed and turning my mental telescope onto old friends in towns that I had left behind. I found, with practice, that I could not only see how they were doing presently, but — like the viewmaster — my telescope could switch backward to show me what kind of week they had had, or forward to see what tomorrow would bring. A sardonic smile would cross my lips as I viewed another day ahead for poor Trudy (five towns back) who would "get it" again from Mrs. Esop for pinching Sammy White's rear in Social Studies.

It seemed that in this calm, restful state of mind, I was capable of getting in touch with the whole world! Bear in mind that the setting was the "Bible belt" Midwest, and I seriously doubt if anyone had ever heard of the word *psychic*. I know that I hadn't. *All I knew then was that I could mentally connect with anyone, at any place and at any hour of the day.*

I began to find that my mental viewmaster and telescope gave me a much clearer and vivid picture of what went on in the history, literature and science books that I was studying in ninth grade. I could feel and see the agony and self-doubts that Abraham Lincoln went through in his childhood years of poverty. I was there when Columbus discovered the New World. My telescope put me "inside" Shakespeare's head as he scripted his verses. There seemed to be no end to what I could look in on — past, present, future. The problem was, of course, in convincing the teachers, the accepted authorities, that I saw and knew much more than they did from their books. Consequently, a good portion of my high school years was spent in the hall or the library doing independent study. . . . The teachers didn't know what to do with my mental viewmaster and telescope.

Years later, I was teaching high school near Hollywood, California. I had entered teaching simply because I wanted to work with the mind, in "bettering it" in some way. As a psychic who had watched others *not* using the full power that they could be using, I was anxious to contribute in whatever way possible to the advancement of the human mind.

It sounded good on paper, but I lasted exactly eight years — teaching languages, at that time the only avenue open, it seemed to me, for a serious believer in the power of the mind to take. Several days into my very first year of teaching, I began to get the sneaking suspicion that public schools were into everything *but* the mind! The discipline, the roll sheets, reports with boxes, reports with fill-in-the-blanks to hand in every time I turned around, everything measured and neatly classified and catalogued — it was too much to bear!

Restless, I began to feel the need to share my expanded world of the mind with my students, who were so bogged down with meeting the demands of paper stacking, paper pushing and paper writing. Feeling equally bogged down, I leveled with them one day: "Do you realize that there is a whole world available at your fingertips that has, as yet, remained unseen by the human eye?"

By their looks, it was apparent that they suspected me of either pushing drugs on the side, or some other wild scheme! But I continued on to explain that they all had a part of them — inside their own minds — that could *enhance* their memories, allow them to mentally "pick up on" the famous people and places they were studying. It could allow them to "see the picture," so to speak, thereby enabling them to gain and retain vital knowledge for their purposes, not only in school, but in everyday life.

I was met with a silence that was about to explode into laughter.

"Stop it!" I demanded. (But they hadn't been doing a thing claimed the class ring leader, who always pleaded innocent.)

"You were thinking!" I blurted, picking up on and annoyed by the class "chemistry" or "air" of thought energy that was not taking me seriously. My last sentence echoed round the classroom. I listened to it, my shoulders starting to shake from laughter. The whole idea of me telling them to stop thinking suddenly hit home with them and with me!

"Progress" and learning were apparently only measurable in terms of boxed-in tests and preconceived notions of what a good student is. *To think* beyond the boundaries of the classroom, while *in* the classroom, God forbid, would be the unpardonable sin. It all seemed so primitive and limiting.

By now, my students and I were all laughing; we were finally on the "same wavelength." I then finished my pitch on the wonders of what their minds could do. They sat up straighter when I mentioned casually that they could use this powerful part of themselves to attract winning conditions in a football game. They could learn to "give off" the right chemistry to get along better with annoying teachers who "had it in for them." They could learn to improve all aspects of their everyday lives, in addition to improving their classroom prowess.

They did, and in practically no time at all. I saw apathetic and sloppy youngsters change into responsible, sharp, and magnetic young adults — people who suddenly had goals and were capable of reaching them, day after day. It was truly exhilarating to watch!

This inspired me to yearn for the day when I could focus solely on teaching the powers of the psychic mind, without the nuisance of other subject matter getting in the way. That day finally came, and in a most unexpected way. A student asked me to tutor him in Spanish. While in the midst of conjugating verbs, he blurted, "Oh, to heck with it! I suppose you already know what I really want, Ms McNeil . . . could you teach me the nitty-gritty of being psychic in everyday events?"

And thus I began my very first mind development "class." It lasted six weeks. And I had perfect attendance, I might add. My student focused on a job that he wanted to "pull in" with the powers of his psychic mind, combined, of course with some practice and footwork. He got the job. He even "pulled in" a lovely girl friend. "And enough money to trade in my old car on a new-used one!" he added. He had bettered his life through his very own psychic powers.

I have spent this past decade teaching men and women around the globe that "you, too, have this beautiful and powerful gift known as the psychic mind." I have witnessed many graduate from lives of want and financial difficulty to lives of increased supply and hap-

14

piness. And this is why I must write this book: The time is right for the word *psychic* to take its proper place in everyday life, where you can make it work for you on a realistic and tangible basis.

1

What Is Psychic?

This book is about your everyday life. It is also about the psychic mind. Now that may sound strange at first. There are many, I am sure, who see *psychic* and *everyday life* as dramatically opposed, having nothing whatsoever to do with each other. The truth is that they can relate to each other, and on a practical day-to-day basis!

Up to and including this century, the concept of psychic power has always been thought of as belonging to a small group of "gifted ones." Psychic powers were relegated to a select group who were touted as having something *special and supernatural* that enable them to see into people, into future possibilities, and feel things that "ordinary people" just don't experience.

As far back as the cave man, through early civilizations, into the Greek and Roman empires, during medieval and Renaissance times, those blessed with psychic powers were used as seers or prophets, issuing predictions, forewarnings and forebodings of events that no one but they could see, events that only they had any power to control with their amazing gift. In both the Eastern and Western worlds, those considered psychic were often kept in the home or royal court by the aristocracy. They served as status symbols to be summoned upon command to tell you whatever you needed to hear at the moment. Keeping a psychic in the house was on the level with keeping good vintage wines in the cellar.

It happens that I am one of "those people," and I shudder to think that, as we head into the twenty-first century, the image of the psychic is still stuck somewhere between the divine throne of God, the gypsy parlor and a good bottle of wine.

The 1960s began a movement of peace-brotherhood-meditation, which expanded into the "self-awareness" groups of the '70s. History will probably look back at the '80s as the decade when the "psychics came out of the parlor." "They're coming out of California! " as one senior citizen put it, and he went on to say that he didn't believe in " 'em." But had I heard? Some well-known psychic had predicted in the tabloids that the entire state of California would plop into the ocean any day now. "Wouldn't want to be out there when that happens!" he added, the crevice between his brows deepening.

No, psychics are not creatures indigenous to California, "land of fruit and nuts," as it is sometimes called. In fact, increasing numbers of psychics the world over are hanging out their shingles and going pro. All well and good. There are some very accurate and, equally important, ethical psychics capable of giving sound advice to make one aware of one's innate possibilities. Note *possibilities*. This leaves the crucial allowance for the client to be in charge of his own life, accepting or rejecting, or applying in his own way the advice of the psychic. Steer clear of the psychic who says, "Like it or not, this is going to happen to you!" ("I sit at the right hand of God and only I can run your life.") Such a person is hardly acting ethically. And by the mere fact that he makes no allowances for human variables, I would question whether he is in fact seeing beyond his own "special" ego. Don't confuse the fortune-teller with the true psychic who *can* transcend the ego and truly "see" and "feel" things.

I remember meeting a so-called psychic, actually a charlatan, at a social event. Befriending me, with too much liquor under her belt, she volunteered one "trick of the trade" that had always impressed her large Italian clientele: "Honey," she slurred, "they're Italian, right? So they gotta have a Tony somewhere in the family! I'm Italian, I've got one!" Aghast, I stared her down as she continued: "So look 'em dead in the eye and whisper: 'Why do I keep hearing the name Tony around you?' If they've got a living Tony, they'll gasp immediately and you've scored points, know what I mean? If they say nothin', then use the family tree bit — somewhere in that cluttered Italian family there's gotta be a Tony. Even if he's been dead two hundred years, that's okay, because now he's a spirit — you get the picture? You can't lose!"

Actually there are ways to tell if a professional psychic is legitimate or not. I hope, after reading this book, you'll not only be able to spot the difference, but more importantly, you will not need to rely or be dependent upon the "gifted powers" of an outsider. And this is where you come in:

You are psychic, too!

You have "the gift!"

But before you make a mad dash to the nearest occult shop for instructions on "how to be one," let me tell you, the occult shop is not the answer. It may offer you bat's blood, magic potions and candles, and perhaps books that tell you how to manipulate and bewitch your lover with your mind. But I cannot emphasize too strongly for the record that none of the above bears any relationship to psychic power. What we are talking about is a positive power that can only be used for ethical purposes, for the highest and best of reasons — such as bettering the lines of communication between you and your spouse, which can enhance and even save a marriage. Manipulation and bewitching smack of ego in charge, not the psychic state of mind. And rest assured; in the next chapter we will get into the basics of how and why you can use your powerful psychic mind.

As we rush towards the year 2000, even the scientific community is confused and in the dark ages as to what-in-blazes a psychic is. Quite obviously, research is needed, but that takes funding and there are those in power who ask, "Why invest all that money in 'the unknown' when we don't know anything about it?"

I have witnessed, as a test subject, the frustrating scientific techniques that try to register accuracy within the standard parameters of laboratory procedure. One such test, which you invariably see in every movie about ESP, involved "tuning in" to a circle, a square or a triangle. As a subject in the next room flipped through some cards, I was to mark the appropriate boxes in front of me. But during that test, stuck in my little isolation booth, I started picking up on the researcher's sex life, another subject's emotions, and the parapsychologist's thoughts about buying a new car. Upon handing in my boxes, I eagerly told this to the parapsychologist in charge, who quipped: "We don't have boxes for emotions and thoughts, Ms McNeil!"

So where does that leave the psychic and his vast unmeasured abilities? Stuck on a primate level, thumbing through ESP cards? I wanted to cry!

I suppose the most humiliating and limiting thing that happened to me as a test subject took place in the lab of a major California university where I was taking part in a federally-funded project on "the psychic." My sensations of another subject's thoughts were to be recorded on tape. Seconds before the test began, I was pulled aside by the psychologist in charge and told in a patronizing voice, "Sandra, dear, we would like to believe your claim that you hear voices, but you must not admit that. Scientists will think you are cuckoo, and that will jeopardize our science grant."

I keep wondering how in heaven's name are we as human beings, who each and every one of us possesses this powerful level of mind, supposed to advance our knowledge of the psychic mind and its potential? How, I wonder, if we are forever held in check by preconceived ideas, myths, and outright fear by those whose programs are funded by skeptics, who have to have everything marked in boxes and explained in terms on a three-dimensional basis.

Don't get me wrong, there are many advances taking place in psychic research even as you read this book. But if research is to advance any further, scientists must allow more scope for the psychic to get beyond the bending of spoons and ESP cards. Having used my psychic ability all my life, sensing its power and potential, I want to shout to the world: *You have the power within you that can enable you to better connect with others and the world about you! Your psychic power can actually make your daily life better!*

Up until now, about the only publications that would print any "proclamations" of a psychic were the tabloids — with headlines that greet you as you check out of your local supermarket: PSYCHIC GRANDMOTHER LEVITATES — PSYCHIC PRIEST BENDS AN ENTIRE SET OF SILVERWARE! More "twaddle," throwing the psychic back into the parlor, and maybe even into the wine cellar again! I once had some material published in those very magazines — at that time the only avenue open to a writer who was an actual psychic. I soon withdrew my name and material from them because of the way in which they showcased my serious intentions — their hype and headlines only made my writings questionable, unfortunately, no matter how documented or how legitimate my credits were. Their approach to the psychic tagged me as something from outer space, to be gawked at.

It is no wonder that the public is confused with so much supernatural hype thrown at them through the tabloids and TV shows that feature various magicians purporting to have "special powers." The powers of the hand? Yes. But the psychic mind as part of their act? Hardly.

I remember one confused lady who wrote me this note: "Dear Ms McNeil, I am in desperate need of a strong *physic*. I hear you're the one to come to."

Then there was the lady pharmacist in Toronto who stopped in the middle of filling my prescription with: "You're the psychic! I'll bet you're dying to hold my ring!" (Actually I felt as if I were dying of influenza at that moment.) But she meant well. Not really sure of what a psychic could do, she didn't know any better. The sad part is that she was potentially psychic, and could have "tuned in" to the very same things that I could have told her!

I also remember the wealthy matron who encountered me on the street and introduced me to her select group of friends: "Ladies, this is my psychic!" As if I were her pet chihuahua! At least a chihuahua could gnash its teeth and growl back at the whole lot of them, caught in some medieval time warp. I could sense that I did not pass the test according to their version of a psychic when one of them remarked to me: "You just don't look a think like a *true* psychic, dear."

Perhaps the most popular image of a psychic is that of one using his special powers to help the police track down runaways and dead bodies. Invariably the first question sprung at me when I do a talk show is: "I suppose you have worked for the police, Ms McNeil." (Pause) "Have you found any dead bodies?"

I am tempted to reply, "Yes. As a matter of fact, I stumbled across three en route to the studio!" Of course, I say nothing of the sort, because I have too much respect for those who are using their psychic abilities to do such good in this area. What I don't have any patience with is the attitude of some authorities and members of the press towards such psychics who, by the way, are seldom if ever paid for their work. (Not being a "legit" occupation in the eyes of many, the psychic is supposed to donate his time and effort out of the spiritual depths of his work day.) Once a psychic has done an accurate job of leading the authorities to dead bodies and what not, some regard the ability to "tune in" as *supernatural*, and set apart from the affairs of everyday life. This makes the psychic come off looking like a cross between a trusty bloodhound who tracks down anything in its path, and God, who sees all and knows all. And, of course — the well-intentioned psychic is regarded as weird and different from us all.

And any publicity in this vein makes the police all the more hesitant to become publicly linked with the psychic, lest the community doubt the police's down-to-earth legitimacy.

Yet the shocking thing is this:

Once you start seeing and experiencing the many functional uses that our psychic mind can perform on a "real" daily basis, you will be able to improve your life, in all areas. Surrounded by the forces of daily stress, economic pressures, puzzling world events, complexities in people, you no longer need to bumble about in the dark, a possible victim as things just happen to you. As an active participant using your own natural mind powers you can become a powerful cause, creating exciting new events in your life! In the chapters that follow you will find easy-to-do techniques that your psychic mind can do to improve everyday situations. *And even change your life!*

Now, let's get at it!

2

Reaching Your Psychic Level of Mind

Just as you were born with a nose for breathing and a heart for pumping blood, so were you born with a mind. Where exactly your mind is located is still a mystery. Neurologists, psychologists, surgeons and chiropractors do, however, agree for the most part on the following evidence found in labs throughout the world.

That part of you that is called the mind is a network of electrically charged circuits that runs throughout your body. According to Chinese medicine, this very energy circulates along various specific pathways in the body that are neurologically connected to specific organs, muscles and nerves.

Exciting new technology has enabled medical doctors and chiropractors to take pictures of the body and its energy circulation. There are numerous scientifically documented books on the market that will tell you that your mind's energies, which run throughout your body, also *radiate outward* from your body, much like radar signals transmitted from a highly charged radar screen. Think of it — you are a walking radar!

Imagine your brain as the switch or control tower of your own radar signals. Scientists have discovered that your brain has at least 150 billion neurons or "power cells," any number of which can be activated when you think a mere thought. With a random thought such as "I'd better go to the store, we need milk," billions of neurons are charged and are signaling nerve impulses that travel as waves of energy, racing throughout your body, and shooting out from your body like flashing signals to the rest of the world. Because the very signals that you give off are electrical, the world about you — being comprised of people with their own "radars" — is actually receiving what you are sending. People may not be *consciously aware* of what they are getting, but they are nonetheless *responding automatically* to what they are picking up on. This is where your powerful psychic level of mind comes into the picture.

Your psychic level of mind is an inner part of you that sees, feels and "picks up on" the energies of others — just as others are getting the very energies that you are constantly putting out. This non-stop exchange of energies exists between us all on this inner level that most people are not even aware of!

As a psychic who is in touch with this exchange of "people-energies" in the air, I am amazed to see that most people go blundering through a day, or through a business meeting, limited to only what they physically hear, what they physically see or touch, while all around them, existing between them and the people they are having to get along with, are tremendously powerful energies. Acting just like telephone wires, their electrical impulses reach and make a connection with the people they are with. *This is where the real business meeting or the real day is happening for a person.* This is where the truest and most intense communication takes place, between you and the rest of the world. It is this level that is picking up, say, that your spouse or friend is tense, that your boss, who took you to lunch, wishes that you would stop talking and just eat. There is an endless supply of daily information available to you. *And above all — helpful.*

Tests at such leading universities as UCLA, Stanford, Alabama, as well as at Oxford in England, have proved that you can reach such a state of awareness, called alpha or subconscious (the words synonymous with psychic), through slowing down, relaxing and simply achieving a passive level of mind.

Most people think that to be psychic and to use any psychic ability, you have to be lying flat on a lab table, hooked up to an EEG machine that registers your brain waves, indicating to you whether or not you are in "alpha," or the psychic level. But realistically, who has the time, the patience, or the directions to the nearest lab site? And if you were hooked up to an EEG machine that proved — yes! There is an altered level at which you can pick up on others — you are likely to do what I did, seconds after reaching that glorious level: I rejoiced! I immediately became so excited at seeing a little light shut off. For my nervousness, my ego and my tensions had shot me back to the normal operating state that we call the *conscious* level.

I personally feel that it's time to place your psychic mind in its true place — in your "real," everyday life, where you can use it in practical, everyday encounters with the human race. And you don't have to have an EEG machine strapped to your head, you don't have to walk around in a trance to perform such feats with your psychic mind while with others.

"Well!" snapped a client. "If I'm so connected with everyone, how come I didn't feel the devious shenanigans that my partner was pulling, when she was pulling them?"

"Because you were not connected to the psychic level within you that was getting " 'the signals.' "

"If I only knew then, I could have done something about it!" droned a businessman whose sales were dropping due to a financial recession. "They're all hanging onto their money, afraid to lose it. And I'm losing my shirt over it!" This man could have looked ahead with his psychic mind and seen that there was going to be a short period of paranoia in the air. Knowing that bit of information ahead of the game, he could have altered his sales pitch to appeal to the needs of those who weren't buying out of fear, and — above all — this man could have planned ahead and prepared for such a possible tight period. So, he wouldn't be a *victim* himself.

"If we're all psychic," quipped a skeptical woman, "then how come none of us have heard of using it until now?"

That is what I keep asking myself again and again. People all over the world have a power so great within them that, operating like a powerful radar, it can put them in touch with anyone at any place and at any time. *It can put them in touch with "what's really going on," not only with others, but with themselves.*

Up until now, you may have been operating in a world limited to your five senses. There has been no need to really put your psychic powers to use. If you have wanted to call and talk with a friend, there

25

was the telephone. You've been able to send a cable or wire to reach someone right away — within the next few hours. The miracles of telex have enabled businesses to "pick up" messages from each other within minutes. All very civilized, physical, and connected to the rest of the world by the boundaries of electrical gadgets. And let us not forget the human mouth, which sometimes goes beyond the boundaries of human decency and the mind's attention span!

As we head into the twenty-first century, we find ourselves facing daily uncertainties — where inflation, taxes and world crises give us the feelings of "Where is it all heading?" — and, "What power do I have over my life?"

SPEAKING OF YOUR POWER

I strongly see and feel that your own psychic level of mind is your *power* that can enable you to "get a handle on things" and take hold of your life, turning it around for the better.

Your psychic level of mind can put you instantly in touch with a loved one's emotions that, up until now, have not been understood — perhaps by either of you. I see many a client who comes to me complaining: "I want so much to communicate with my husband (or wife), but he just won't cooperate. He's in some kind of shell." In taking a psychic look at the situation, I see that indeed there is a shell around the spouse. And the client hasn't the foggiest idea of why it got there, or how to remove it. This is where the psychic mind comes in — it is a pure channel of energy that runs from each of us to the other. In learning how to tap into it, that client could not only learn what the problem was, but could restore the flow of love once more.

Your psychic level of mind can connect you with associates the day before a meeting and let you feel them out as to where they stand on crucial issues, ethics (or lack of), and on you. Horrified, I once watched a high-powered salesman turn off a group of clients in the next booth to me at a restaurant. It seemed that Mr. Salesman-of-the-Decade was so impressed with his voice and the pitch he was delivering that he lost touch with the group he was talking to. I could actually see that he had never been in touch, because he had not been in touch with "what was really going on" with them. It was as clear as day and night to me, as I tuned in: the group simply wanted him to stop. He had made his point. And by the way, quite well.

They had listened with interest. But the man did not know when to shut up.

Your psychic level of mind can put you mentally in touch with the flow of the day ahead of you, giving you a general, even specific idea of how the day ahead looks — with its possibilities. How many times have you been surprised at what you encountered during your day?

"Oh, but I don't want to see anything bad!" whined the lady in my seminar, making a face.

"Then don't," I replied. "Through techniques that you choose and learn, you can limit or control the various possibilities that you see." I then went on to relate some case histories of myself and other people who did in fact avoid negative and "bad" situations, due to our "picking up on" those very possibilities ahead of time. You can open yourself to seeing a clear and total picture of anything — putting yourself *in power* as you become aware and "up" for any such possiblity. That puts you "one up" on others, who might not be in touch at all with their psychic senses, or, if they are, they are limiting the picture and signals of what to do by trying to put a clamp on the very power that could help them.

WHAT YOU MUST KNOW BEFORE YOU USE YOUR PSYCHIC LEVEL OF MIND

Without your circuit of mind energies, you would be just a slab of meat. There would be no emotions, no thoughts, no energy at all. You would have no aura. You would have no magnetism. There would be nothing radiating from you.

With the mind energies that move through you and surround you, you become a walking ball of energy. This energy is not only electrical, but it is magnetic, attracting to it and to you the same energies of others, resulting in certain people being attracted to you because of "a certain something within you." This electromagnetic ball of energy is the stuff that you are made of. Perhaps the kinds of thoughts that you have been thinking lately have been signaling and attracting the wrong people to you. Rest assured, one random thought hasn't much, if any, power. It is what your thoughts dwell on that really sends electrical signals to the rest of the world.

Some research has been done on "taking pictures" of this powerful force field that the human body gives off. One of the means of seeing such a force field has been through the process of Kirlian photography, a controversial photo-plate method that records, then emits a picture of light around the human hand, for example, as the subject thinks thoughts, feels emotions or falls alseep. As a test subject of this process at UCLA, I found that whenever my emotions changed, so did the "color" and even intensity of the energy that I was giving out. In a "down" mood one day, my mind wandered to a fun vacation that I was about to take. Suddenly, the aura or energy field around my hand changed from a murky gray to a bright, white glow. (I, by the way, had just come from doing my taxes.) It not only was shooting outward in long, strong arrow-like strokes, but I noticed that the air had changed in the lab. The assistants around me started to chatter with more lightness to their tone. I could feel them reacting to me more positively than when I had come in just a few minutes before, literally carrying a murky cloud around me. Not being a scientist, I am not endorsing this method of photography. I am just reporting that as my force field's color changed to white, indicative of positive flow, so did a "good air" connect me with those in the room. How many times have you found yourself in a good mood for whatever reasons, with the rest of the world smiling back at you? And have you ever been at work or at home, feeling down, encountering a bad day, with people rubbing you the wrong way? Think of this — it could be that in your down and negative state, you were literally rubbing against or conflicting with the energies of those around you who put up their guard against your negative energies. All of this takes place on the psychic level of mind, where, had you not been in touch with what was going on, you might have written yourself off as "nobody likes me anymore." Your psychic mind could have told you this would happen. And it would have let you know that this bad day would pass.

Every time you psychically "pick up on" the world about you, the energies that surround your body as your neurological "network" form openings. These openings are often called *chakras*, a Sanskrit term that means revolving wheel.

Doctors, chiropractors, and neurologists may not all use the word *chakra*, yet they acknowledge the fact that the human body is a network of energy circuits, which do, in fact, have focal points of power — being the *chakra* centers. These power centers are neurologically "hooked up" to the vital organ centers, as well as to the *Total Energy Flow*, or *prana* (meaning life energy). California chiropractor Dr. Tom Chappell successfully combines X-ray information with his expertise in body structure in treating his patients, as do many physicians and chiropractors the world over. Dr. Chappell is among a new breed of medical expert, who not only does X rays for the *standard* checkup, but uses the photographed pictures of energy from those X rays in becoming aware of "just who his patient is," and "how he works" — according to energy flow that is captured on X-ray plates. Like so many medical experts, Dr. Chappell acknowledges the fact that the body's energies move in circuits — with those circuits arriving at central "power centers" known as *chakras.*

The *chakras* — your energy power centers — can be opened, enabling you to receive and send energies to a greater extent with your psychic mind: your *chakras* are like valves that open and close — allowing your neurological network of mind energies to keep a steady flow or *exchange* of signals between your psychic level and the outside world. Just as your lungs pump in and out, so could it be said that your *chakras* do the same — and just as you don't worry about the functioning of your lungs, so should you not concern yourself with how your *chakras* are doing!

Once you start opening up to your psychic power, you will find that the entire process flows automatically — making you feel at home while doing the exercises. A reminder: at first, however, you may not feel as if anything is happening! — and that is a natural sensation — after all, you have been told that your psychic mind is *all powerful,* and as you sit doing the exercise, you don't feel any sensation association with such grandiose power! Your *all powerful* psychic mind, being a natural process, will *take charge* in a natural and automatic way — just as your powerful heart or powerful brain move powerfully and regularly *despite* any overwhelming sensations that you may feel related to them. For any other exercises to be effective, you must — as in all things worth their weight in gold — give them a chance. And keep at them. If you don't see results in three days, keep on! You may see results, however, on the first day. Great! If not, it simply means that you need more time. Your psychic mind, like a muscle, will naturally bring stronger results for you, the more you exercise it!

The mistake a lot of people make upon trying to get into their psychic level is that they feel that they *must* get there — "do or die!" Their ego becomes the predominant factor, causing frustration, tension, and unrest — and presto — no psychic level! This is mainly because the psychic mind, which is passive and beyond the realm of the ego, becomes out of reach for them.

If you are starting out — never having done much work with your psychic mind, I advise that you take it all nice and easy — not worrying a bit if you can't get into the mood, or can't get the feel of the exercise on the first try — or even on the first few tries. Developing the powers of your psychic mind is like learning how to walk: it is all a natural process that merely comes to you with practice. Remember how it was when you tried to take your first few steps? You fell, I'll wager. Your muscles, your attention span, and your over-all movement was shaky. You were too conscious of failing (or falling!) to succeed and walk. Once you got to practicing daily, you finally developed a spontaneous feel for walking — just as you will from "developing the muscles of your mind" through your psychic exercises. And in time, you'll move and maneuver as naturally as you walk.

And another point to remember: the very things and situations that you mentally program for — if they are worth anything at all — just don't come at the snap of a finger. Some do not come overnight. If you do the exercises faithfully, don't give up if what you are programming for has not "arrived." The more complex and great the "goal," often times the longer it can take. So, stay focused, and be ready. Opportunities come when there is someone — such as yourself — who is ready in mind and spirit. Keep mentally focusing on everything you are aiming for — in the way of *creative visualization*, and in the right time, those very substances will be aiming for your life.

The following diagram will give a basic idea of where your energy *chakras* are in relation to the rest of your body.

The more relaxed a person is, the more his energy centers or *chakras* will be open to the flow of psychic information.

Now it's simply a matter of relaxing.

The pressure is on, so you're tensing up, right? Actually, there is a simple but effective way to cause your bodily rhythms to slow down and the *chakras* to open naturally. The technique below uses effective breathing strategies, which are as old as time.

YOUR BASIC *CHAKRAS*

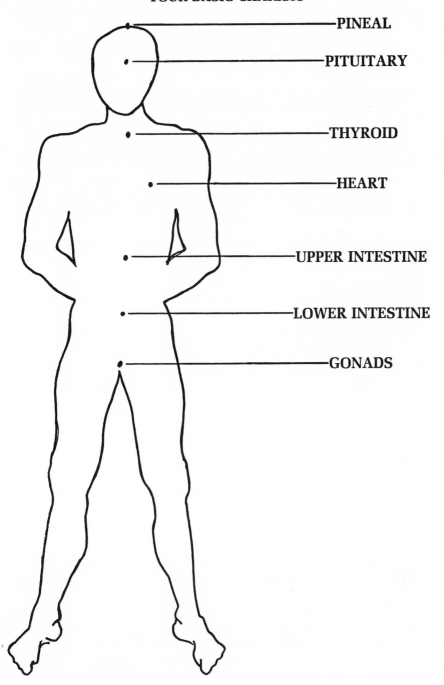

PINEAL

PITUITARY

THYROID

HEART

UPPER INTESTINE

LOWER INTESTINE

GONADS

EASY STEPS TO RELAXATION

In a comfortable sitting position, do the following:

Step 1 Close your eyes and take in a deep breath through your nostrils, puffing out your body to the count of 1 – 2 – 3, envisioning yourself to be a gigantic air-filled balloon. Tense up and hold that breath. Release the air through your nostrils and mouth, commanding all tensions and worries to be falling away from you with each particle of air that you let out. Repeat two more times.

Step 2 Close your eyes and turn your head to the left, taking a deep breath through the nostrils. Hold it. Then turn your head to the right, releasing your breath through the nostrils and mouth, feeling all tensions and negativity working their way out of your body. Repeat this two more times. Now reverse and turn your head to the right, taking in a deep breath. Hold it. Now turn your head to the left, releasing your breath through the nostrils and mouth. Repeat two more times. This exercise passes air circulation through your lungs, cleansing you and relaxing the nervous system.

Step 3 Clasping your hands behind your neck, point your head downward toward your lap to the count of 1 – 2. Raise your head. Place your hands on your lap. Take a moment in the quiet to envision yourself surrounded in a shower of warm and soothing white light.

When a person reaches the psychic level of mind, the energy *chakras* will be open and ready to receive and send mental energies from mind to mind. I have found that there is a way to manipulate your *chakras* to open to their fullest. Such manipulation is achieved only by means of positive suggestions that you give your mind, thereby achieving only positive results in opening your *chakras* at will.

By focusing on certain colors, whose vibrations directly resemble the vibrations of each energy *chakra*, you can cause each *chakra* to open to a greater extent than usual. Below is a list of the *chakras* and the colors to focus on in order to open each *chakra* to its fullest extent.

CHAKRAS	FOCUS COLOR
PINEAL	VIOLET
PITUITARY	BLUE
THYROID	BLUE
HEART	GREEN
UPPER INTESTINE	YELLOW
LOWER INTESTINE ᵕ	ORANGE
GONAD	RED

ARE THERE LIMITS TO WHAT YOU CAN DO WITH YOUR POWERFUL PSYCHIC MIND?

Yes. Straight and simple: when it comes to using your psychic mind to hurt anyone or manipulate them into doing something negative against their will. Such a "power trip" would not work, for basically simple reasons.

Your psychic level of mind is passive and beyond the grip of the ego, which is the part of you that would be involved in anything intentionally or unintentionally harmful to or manipulative of others in a negative way. Why? Because when you do a negative turn to someone, intentionally or even unintentionally harming them, you are operating against the flow of divine or cosmic goodness and positive energies. Negativity is not the state of the psychic mind, which only can be found in a positive divine light. Because the psychic mind is your only real power, it is therefore only "working with power" when you use it for the highest and best of reasons. You might want to use it to compete for a job. That is fine. We live in a world where natural competition is healthy. But to use it to "zap" someone so that he will drop out of the race will only create a boomerang effect, zapping *you* in the end.

Back to the lab where I took part in Kirlian experiments: I found that if I envisioned the color *white* or lightness in general, my actual force field would change colors from dark to light. And the more positive I felt, the more that very white appeared time after time. Many parapsychologists have noted that the color white, the most potent of the spectrum, is directly related to *positive forces* emitted from the human mind, or positive energy, in general. Throughout this book, I will suggest that you "put a white light around yourself." Upon hearing this, don't stick your head under the nearest lamp shade. Merely envision, with eyes shut or open, the effect of a white shower of light pouring down around you, creating around you a powerful and positive force field that *enhances* your power all the more!

As a subject I have done Kirlian experiments to envision negative thoughts toward another. My force (registering murky) not only could not reach the target subject, but it curled backward, shooting right back at me. On the days in which I practised my negative thoughts in a lab set-up, I experienced heavy problems with people in everyday life when I left the lab.

So I assure you, your psychic mind is a positive force that can *only* do positive things for you. And I can't stress enough that the positive things that your psychic mind is capable of can be astounding at times, as well as being just plain helpful in daily situations.

REACHING YOUR PSYCHIC MIND

The Steps:

1   Close your eyes and take in a deep breath through your nostrils, puffing out your body. Hold it. Now release, imagining all the air shooting out the top of your head and forming a gigantic white parachute.

2   Tell yourself to relax and drift . . . relax and drift . . . relax and drift with your beautiful white parachute pulling you along with not a care in the world.

3   Feel yourself plunging gently into warm pools of water whose energy vibrations directly open and relax your *chakras*:
    – Plunge into a warm pool of blue water and relax in it
    – Plunge into a warm pool of green water and relax in it
    – Plunge into a warm pool of yellow water and relax in it
    – Plunge into a warm pool of orange water and relax in it
    – Plunge into a warm pool of red water and relax in it

4   Feel yourself being pulled down a long, red tunnel whose energies are connecting you with your own gut level, or psychic mind. Count down from ten to one, and imagine yourself to be floating smoothly down your own pipeline to the psychic mind. The

closer to one you get, the more in tune and relaxed you will feel.

5 On the count of one envision yourself to be in your psychic level of mind. See it as a plain white room that contains a white overstuffed easy chair and a workbench in front of that chair. The workbench is where you cause positive things to happen in your daily life.

6 Feel yourself climbing into the chair. Relax and know that the positive images you focus on down here are connecting forces that reach out to the people and situations in your life on the physical plane.

7 Take a moment and envision a miniature of yourself on your workbench. See and feel yourself to be the *picture of success*. See yourself smiling. Physically smile along with this. This active involvement with you-as-success activates and projects billions of nerve energies from your *chakras* within seconds.

8 Know that at any time you can come to this powerful level of your mind, tune into others, tune into your own daily life, or connect with anyone and any situation.

9 When you are ready to return to the external conscious level merely count from one to three and command yourself to be wide awake — wide awake.

This exercise is one of many approaches that I use in getting in touch with the powerful psychic level of mind. Once you reach this level, which becomes easier with practice, you will then be able to get down to putting psychic mind energies to work in your daily life.

In the chapters to come, you will be shown mental exercises that will connect you in better ways with loved ones, and connect you with the work-a-day world in which you must function effectively. The exercises ahead of you are easy to follow, yet powerful. They will put you in touch with your own psychic power, a force so magnetic that it can attract to you specific situations and people that you focus on.

Your psychic level of mind is a super thing. It can perform wonders for you. And it is a natural thing: it is an integral part of you, functioning naturally on a daily basis. Now it is a simple and natural matter to reach it. *Natural mind power is at your fingertips.*

Use it and start to see positive results in your daily life!

3

Preparing Yourself For Success

The people around you are automatically responding to you, relating to the psychic signals that you are giving off. Let's say, for example, you are trying to give an impression of confidence and authority as you apply for the job of personnel director for a large, prestigious firm. The interviewer looks at your résumé, then at you. You have the right credentials. You physically look the part. Yet something is wrong: the interviewer casts you a luke-warm smile, telling you he has to see a few more people before making up his mind. You automatically nod in agreement. As you leave his office, something tells you: "Nothing will come of this. I'm not worth it."

The interviewer was also in agreement with your attitude long before it came to the surface! It was within you. You were giving it off from your psychic energy base, and the interviewer was psychically receiving it. He reacted accordingly. In his conscious mind he might have found himself thinking: "There's something about this person that is not right for the job." You were a victim of your own psychic signals. We are constantly exchanging psychic signals between our respective energy bases.

Here is a shocking truth that most people are unaware of. Your psychic energy base contains not only current thoughts, feelings and emotions, but it contains the thoughts, feelings and emotions of all that you have been through to date. Presently, you may be projecting a wonderful self-image. You like yourself. You are hopeful about the future. But what about all those thoughts and energies that were yours in the past . . . your doubts, fears, your inability to like yourself? There was a time in your life when you felt that nobody liked you. You were overweight, you felt ugly, and were sure that people avoided you like the plague. At that time in your life, those negative energies became an integral part of your psychic energy base. There they remained, following you to the present. Even though newer, more positive thoughts now occupy your self-image, those old energies could nonetheless still be within you, a part of the psychic signals that you are transmitting to others, who are automatically responding to your total psychic signals. They could be treating you as less-than-wonderful because they are automatically reacting to old energies . . . that old rotten self-image buried deep within your psychic energy base.

"Jeepers!" snapped a paranoid lady, in the middle of my lecture. "I'm afraid to think a thought!"

"You just thought one!" ("Boo!") Then I added, to the relief of many: One random thought is like one bite of junk food. Only if it is the only thing you focus on will it stay with you.

What you focus on is the foundation of your energy base.

The following psychic energy base is one that I saw with my own psychic mind when looking in on a thirty-five-year-old salesman who seemed to be feeling great insecurities "for no reason," as he put it — especially when he had to pitch his products to authority figures in charge of large companies. It is obvious that this individual was still carrying around old negativity that was standing in the way of new success.

There is a lot to the adage: *"A chain is only as strong as its weakest link."* If you are still carrying around old energies of "I can't," "I'm not worth it" or "Nothing good ever happens to me," then it is certain that your success potential is weakened by these negative factors in your psychic energy base.

"Yes, but that's the way I used to think back in college," exclaimed a client to me one day. "I'm okay now!" In taking a psychic look at his energy base, I could see that he was "okay" until he had to entertain out-of-town clients for dinner. Then he "happened" to develop a cold or a sore throat, which prevented him from socializing

DIAGRAM OF HUMAN PSYCHIC ENERGY BASE

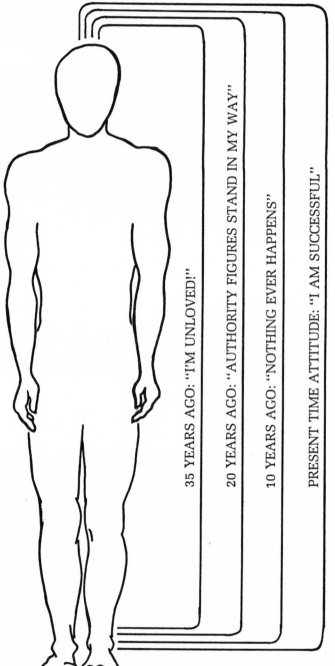

35 YEARS AGO: "I'M UNLOVED!"

20 YEARS AGO: "AUTHORITY FIGURES STAND IN MY WAY"

10 YEARS AGO: "NOTHING EVER HAPPENS"

PRESENT TIME ATTITUDE: "I AM SUCCESSFUL"

"A Thirty-five-year-old Salesman"

Chakras, or "transmitters," that conduct constant exchange of *psychic signals* between this person and others.

at all. Taking a further look at his energy base, I could see that my client was still carrying around old fears and insecurities, which he had picked up when, years ago, he had socialized for weeks trying to make a college fraternity, only to be rejected. At the time he felt like a complete failure. He created the self-image of "I'm not good at socializing. I'm a reject." I mentioned to my client what I saw in his past. His jaw dropped, and he admitted: "So that's why every business dinner always triggers fear of failing." Without knowing it, my client had been a victim of past energies that were interfering with present success!

When I visit Los Angeles, I often see actor or actress clients. Some of the beginners find it so hard to get a movie part, much less an agent. "Why isn't anything happening for me?" they ask. In taking a psychic look at their energy bases, I see that their focus is on the wrong thing. They are still seeing themselves as "hopefuls" or "nobodies" or "just beginners," as they will often refer to themselves. Think of the signals that they must be giving out — "I'm not *really* an actor, so why should you hire me?" The end result is that nobody does.

Even though you may not be quite the success that you want to be, start *focusing* on yourself as that very success, especially when in your psychic level of mind, and the impact upon the rest of the world, and your own life, will be felt immediately.

I know a housewife who wins many, varied contests simply by *focusing on herself as the winner* while in the psychic level of mind. Then when she steps out into her day as an office clerk, she carries with her that air of success that is pulling to her not only her prize winnings, but a better day in general.

"Oh, no," moaned a concerned man, interrupting my lecture on prosperity. "What if we all become positive and powerful and focus on the same thing?"

"What do we do?" burst in a paranoid businessman. "Shoot anybody who looks positive?"

Laughter interrupted them both, followed by some serious thinking. What if we all developed our "special powers" to know, understand and be in tune with one another?

Another kind of laughter erupted — one of sudden insight: If we all are more positive and "in tune" with events and people than we are now, so much the better for all concerned!

But what if we all compete for the same thing? What if 250 men and women — all projecting the wonders of natural mind power —

up and apply for the same job position with a large company with only one position open. Who would get it then? *They can't all be hired for the same job!* What would happen?

The one best attuned to the highest and best of powers within him would win over the other "natural mind power people." And what about them? Would they be left out in the cold?

Absolutely not!

Once you tap into the powers of your psychic mind — which is like a radar beam — you start broadcasting to the world that you are ready for equal or better success to come your way. Of course, you don't go home, lock your doors, pull the shades and wait for S-U-C-C-E-S-S to knock on your door. You proceed, you persevere, but you don't get panicky, and you don't settle for defeat. You keep doing the psychic exercises and keep walking your path — knowing that you too are a winner and are bound "to pull in" the equivalent of what you "put out" — if not *this* time, then at the right time for you!

Above all remember: there is room in the universe for everybody. No crowding is necessary! You can't lose when you activate your special powers of the psychic mind!

A LOOK AT YOUR ENERGIES

Your thoughts, feelings and emotions over the years are fed into a computer-like file system that stores all information in your psychic energy base. The *you* walking around right now is the sum total of all data you have received to date.

I am not saying that it is wrong to have a computerized data system within you. Accumulating energies is a natural function. What I am saying, however, is this: You could be carrying around within you specific data that are holding you back from present and future success.

ARE YOU A VICTIM OF OLD ENERGIES?

Here are some signposts that will tell you that perhaps you are a victim of past thoughts, past feelings or past programming.

1 If you are forever repeating a romantic pattern that upsets or leaves you with a bad feeling about yourself.

*You keep attracting the same kind of love interests only to find out too late that they are class-A jerks. They all appear to treat you alike. They verbally abuse you. They lie. They cheat on you.

They drop you for someone else. They fail to notice your good points and, by this time, you question whether you have any good points at all.

*You keep finding yourself beginning and ending relationships, without rhyme or reason.

*You find yourself avoiding commitments.

*You find yourself reacting to the opposite sex in an automatic way that makes you feel uneasy, yet you keep doing it.

*You hold strong views regarding "what is wrong" with the opposite sex.

*Most members of the opposite sex make you angry, fearful or feel down, because they remind you of a parent.

*The opposite sex is constantly reacting to you in a recognizable pattern.

*The opposite sex reacts to you the way it did several years ago.

*Whenever an argument arises between you and your spouse or love interest, you panic for no reason.

2 If you tend to attract more than your share of career delays, snags, problems in general.

*You find yourself reacting to persons of authority much the same way that you reacted to parents and teachers.

*You can't seem to shake the feeling that you are not worthy of success.

*You find yourself feeling vague fears about loss of job, for no reason.

*You believe that success cannot come until you have suffered sufficiently.

*If you encounter good news related to career matters, you find yourself automatically thinking: "So what's the catch?"

*There are certain types of individuals who make you feel inferior.

*No matter how you behave, your co-workers treat you with no respect.

*You cannot seem to hold down a job.

*Just as soon as you arrive at a successful plateau, you start feeling vague fears of "this can't last forever."

3 If money seems to be a constant problem with you.

*You experience vague worries about losing your shirt or being out on the street though this has never happened to you.

*You feel that money is nasty and dirty, and you feel guilty about admitting your goal is to make a lot of it.

*You feel guilty about making money without struggle and punishment of some kind.

*Money seems hard to come by, despite your efforts and hard work.

*Just as soon as you bring in some extra money, it goes out as quickly, due to sudden emergencies that crop up.

4 If your physical body seems to act up for no reason at all.

*You seem to come down with a mysterious ailment every time a certain type of situation arises.

*You have a chronic condition that keeps you from doing certain things.

*You feel queasy at the thought of seeing certain people, at the thought of going to certain places.

*Just when everything seems to be going your way, you always seem to develop a cold or the flu.

*Good news or success makes you feel light-headed, as well as uneasy.

Don't try to match the events of your life with the above list. But if you have ever felt similar feelings in situations of your own, then perhaps you could be carrying around old negatives that need to get cleared out.

Hypnotherapists at such leading hospitals as UCLA and Sloan-Kettering in New York have found in working with their patients that it is very possible to clean out old data from your subconscious mind, the core of your psychic energy base. You may even choose to be in therapy to improve your self-image. If so, the psychic mind exercises in this book can only aid or supplement the outside help you are getting. Many people find, however, that once they tap into their own psychic potential to deal with the negatives and problems at hand, they experience no need to seek outside help. That decision, like all decisions, is yours to make.

Your psychic level is the *computerized part of you* that can get rid of old negatives that perhaps have been holding you back. Just as your psychic level, or subconscious, has taken in and stored your energies over the years, so can it get rid of the energies that you select.

"But what if I don't know what to get rid of?" is the common question.

Your subconscious has everything on file and knows what is what, just as a computer keeps on file the helpful data separated from the old data that are outdated.

By merely doing an exercise to place you in touch with your psychic energy base, you will be priming your subconscious, or psychic level, to automatically delete negative data. It is sufficient to know that you do have negatives to release.

GETTING IN TOUCH WITH YOUR PSYCHIC ENERGY BASE

The Steps:

1 Go to your psychic level of mind, as demonstrated in Chapter Two.

2 Get into your overstuffed white easy chair and command yourself to be *relaxed*.

3 Imagine this room as cool, dark and very peaceful.

4 Command your mind to create a picture of your psychic energy base, all around you, like a swirling white tornado surrounding your entire body.

5 Mentally say: "*I am in touch with my psychic energy base!*" Take a few moments in the quiet to *feel* any feelings, hunches or thoughts that come to mind. They may just pop in and out of your mind without making sense at the time. Or you may find yourself

getting actual "guidance" or awareness of what is within you. Either can take place. But one thing is for certain. As you accept the fact that you are in touch with your own psychic energy base, so are you programming yourself to feel at least a general awareness — if not immediately, then at a later time.

6 When you feel that you have had enough for now, return to your conscious level by counting to three.

The more that you practise getting in touch with your own psychic energy base, as in all the exercises in this book, the more you will develop a *feeling* for what you are hooking up with.

I have personally witnessed men and women who have been victims of their vague fears, depressions, and troublesome situations which they cannot "logically figure out," preventing them from getting anywhere.

They can simply do an exercise in which they command their computer to "dump away" any and all negativity in their psychic level of mind. This can condition their neurological circuits of energy that contain fears and thoughts of defeat, so that they create a flow of positive, improved energies running through their *core*. Call it self-hypnosis, call it positive imagery. It is your psychic mind giving *more power to you and to your individual life.*

DUMPING AWAY OLD NEGATIVES THAT HAVE BEEN HOLDING YOU BACK

This exercise might seem a bit silly. However, it has been proved that *the more exaggerated and even outlandish your thoughts, so much greater is the impression upon your own mind.*

The Steps:

1 Find a comfortable sitting position. Relax and close your eyes.

2 Imagine a beautiful white light all around you to insure you of sound, positive energies.

3 Command yourself to see a garbage can. It is gray, it is vile, and it is dirty. In fact, it stinks! Written across it in bold red letters is the word TRASH. This is a symbol to your mind that you are dumping old garbage from your life. Remember: your subconscious mind believes what you feed it, be it fact or exaggeration.

4 Feel yourself (do this with your physical hands) *dumping all negativity into the garbage can.* You may not be able to recall all you "need to get rid of," but your psychic computer, or subconscious, knows and does it for you automatically. Now, *put a lid on it* — a symbol of it "being taken care of."

5 Embrace the garbage can. Now, you can release yourself from all negativity.

6 *Dramatically drop your arms from the garbage can* and command yourself to *feel the relief* of letting go of all negativity — past and present. Mentally say: *"I let go of all negativity."*

7 When you wish, command yourself to be *wide awake* and *feeling such relief!* — knowing that all has been taken care of by your powerful psychic computer.

I have had many people remark: "When I use my psychic mind, I feel hooked up not only to my own inner power, but to *something far greater than myself.*" I have no explanation. But I sense that in hooking up to your psychic radar systems, you do indeed "hook up" to vast, positive forces — "divine forces," as many call them, that add more power to you, to your loved ones, and to your life.

If you practice the exercise to get in touch with your psychic energy base over a period of time, it is certain that you will start to get a feeling for what energies, thoughts and emotions you should plan on dumping. If nothing comes to mind for a while, it doesn't mean you have failed. Perish the thought! *That* kind of energy you can do without. It simply means that the information is still locked within the limits of your subconscious mind. As your psychic level, or subconscious, is a storehouse of information, you're simply *making contact with it* and can get the answers, the guidance, the feelings that you need to help you with your life.

Your subconscious computer behaves, then, according to what it is fed. When you command it to *release old negatives holding me back,* it kicks in powerful energies that obey your mental command. This action leaves your psychic energy base with a more positive, more success-prone you. *You have cleared the decks of all negatives.* All systems are "go" for success!

GETTING RID OF SPECIFIC NEGATIVES

Perhaps there are specific negatives that are keeping you from being the kind of person that you want to be. You might even be aware that these very energies and negative self-doubts are holding you back from any new success. Yet you keep having the same doubts, fears, and feelings — finding yourself attracting to you the same negative situations.

I'll call this the *yes-but syndrome*. A perfect example of it is an account of what a client of mine was going through.

He had just survived a divorce and bankruptcy. He was depressed and saw no future for himself. He came to me for hope, I suppose. In taking a psychic look at what his possibilities were in the upcoming weeks, I could clearly see that he could "pull in" some new opportunities. But he would have to develop a positive focus on them all, or they might not happen *then*. I also mentioned to him that he was a *yes-but* victim, still clinging to old thoughts of limitation and fear of failure.

"Yes, but," came the reply, "I have just come from bankruptcy, divorce, depression. . . ." He droned on and on, giving me every reason under the sun *why* he should be a failure, instead of a success. *This man was programmed to hold onto failure.*

In taking a further look at his psychic energy base, I could see that his father had badgered him when he was a boy about not being able to "play with the big boys one day" if he ever went into business for himself. The father thought the boy lazy and powerless. The boy was forever getting bullied by kids on the block, which made the father spout off such statements as: "You think you're pushed around now! Wait till you get older!" Of course the father, a businessman fighting the system, was also also venting his fears of seeing his own flesh and blood growing up to be a powerless carbon copy of himself. The young boy didn't know the difference. To him, and particularly to his psychic computer, they were fed data that said: *You are a failure, particularly as you grow older and try to deal with the "big boys."* I mentioned my awareness of this to him, and he began to cry. He told me that the past year had found him in one situation after another where he had had to deal with successful businessmen, or, as he put it, "the big boys." Because he was *programmed to fail* in such a situation, he found his business going bankrupt. Such turbulence had spilled over into the home, where his marriage of ten years had fallen apart.

This story, I must add, has a happy ending. I asked him if he wanted to change his life. Looking at me as if I had a few loose screws, he nodded yes and waited for my advice — a simple statement — that he had negative things on file within him that he needed to get rid of. I gave him an exercise and bid him good luck as he disappeared through the doorway. Six weeks later I received a call from him. He reported that not only had his feelings about himself started to improve, but so had his life as well. He had "pulled in," as he put it, a new job with a successful new company that was letting him be his own boss.

When I saw him again, he was not the same person who had seen me weeks before. He had cleaned his files of old negativities. He was now the psychic energy base of success, and it showed!

If you are presently in a situation where you want to improve your life, but a little voice keeps reminding you "yes, but remember grim realities," then perhaps you are being held back by old files that should be gotten rid of.

This next exercise, *cleaning your files,* can be used as a general cleaning exercise instead of, or in addition to, *the garbage-can technique.* You are in control and can select, and even alter to your liking and use, the exercises in this book. For example, you may not want to say the affirmation that I have given. Then make up a powerful one that you feel good with.

When you do the next exercise and are aware that there are definite specifics that must be gotten rid of, command that *you are now getting rid of them.* You really don't have to know the specifics. The important thing is that you accept that you are now ridding yourself "of specifics holding you back" — whatever they may be. Your powerful psychic computer does the rest.

CLEANING YOUR FILES

The Steps:

1 Go to your psychic level of mind as directed in Chapter Two.

2 Climb into your white overstuffed easy chair.

3 On your work table in front of you envision a miniature replica of yourself. (If you can't see it fully, remember that your computer is making that energy happen anyway so don't worry.)

4 See your image on the table developing an actual file cabinet in the stomach area.

5 Feel yourself reaching for this file cabinet and pulling out a drawer where your files are kept. (Act this out with your hands for more impact.) Even though your conscious mind might think: "This is silly," your computer will automatically be preparing you for emptying your files of negativity.

6 Feel your fingers going above the files, and mentally say: "I am automatically getting rid of specific negatives that have been holding me back!"

Option: If you are aware of what specifics you need to get rid of as you place your fingers above the files, mentally feel yourself getting rid of specifics, saying, "I am automatically getting rid of these specific negatives" (list them).

7 Command yourself to feel relief at being cleared of specific negatives.

8 Wake up on the count of three.

Whether you like it or not, you are a creature of thought. And up until now you have perhaps been letting any thought, worry or doubt occupy your mind, to say nothing of occupying your psychic energy base. It would be unrealistic to expect you, a human, to never think a negative thought again. After all, you are in the mainstream of life, in day-to-day encounters with people, some of whom may not be all that positive or nice to do business with. And what if you encounter a real jerk who gives you a rough time at work? Do you smile sweetly and blow a kiss his way? Or stick out your tongue, then dump your tongue in the garbage can? Or do you think nothing?

Actually, you do none of the above. The rest of this book will be devoted to showing you how to overcome specific situations by using the powers of your psychic level of mind. In the meantime, if you suspect that your energy base could use a good cleaning, then simply do the garbage can exercise. If you suspect that certain specific thoughts about yourself are keeping you from succeeding, then clean your files! Get rid of the old *at any time*. If you are one of those persons who is constantly on the go, leaving little time to ponder about your psychic energy base, take a few moments from time to time to dump any and all general negatives into your garbage can, releasing the old for good.

Any thought or feeling, of course, that you tend to dwell upon or worry about is bound to make more of an impression or imprint upon your computer.

What about the negatives that just pop up from time to time? I mentally image the word(s) or thought "in a white cloud" as I mentally say: "*I release this thought!*"

If you are a victim of constant worries, doubts or fears that you cannot seem to shake, then here are some exercises to enable you to "take away" such specific negative imprints from your computer.

DEPROGRAMMING YOURSELF OF WORRIES

The Steps:

1 In a sitting position, get comfortable, close your eyes.

2 Create an image of yourself in front of you. This image is standing on a white sheet (suggestive of a positive base). This sheet has a black border, suggesting a *magnet* that all negatives will be pulled to.

3 See your arms stretched out to each side.

4 As you command "I let go of all negative worries" see an iron filing effect of black specks flying away from your body and hooking up with the black border. Suddenly see the black border disappear, with only the white positive left.

5 Awaken to the count of 1 – 2 – 3 knowing that all is well

DEPROGRAMMING YOURSELF OF RECURRING DOUBTS

*Do exactly the same steps in this exercise as you did with the previous one.

*When you get to the command part, say: "*I let go of all negative doubts.*"

*Proceed with the exercise, the same way you did in the previous one.

DEPROGRAMMING YOURSELF OF RECURRING FEARS

*Do exactly the same steps as in the previous two exercises.

*When you get to the command part, say: "*I let go of all negative fears.*"

*Proceed as you did with the other two exercises.

Of course, as with any exercises in this book, you can choose one exercise over another for a specific problem. Let's say that you want to be freed from chronic fears of aging and death. You have the option of doing the garbage can exercise, the file-cleaning exercise, or the last exercise where you are deprogramming your fears in a specific approach. The choice is yours to make; you are in the driver's seat.

The next chapter will deal with daily negatives that you may encounter — what to do about them, how to react to them, and above all, how to project a powerful and positive *you* that can overcome and sail right through the negatives that tend to hold you back.

Nothing can stop you once your computer is programmed for success!

4

How To Deal With Negatives

"It would be easy to think good thoughts if I didn't have the mortgage and those god-awful bills hanging over my head!" exclaimed a father of four. Change the person and the line a bit, and you might find yourself having the same type of feeling at one time or another.

How many times have you started out the day with high hopes, only to encounter the irritating moods of others? This brings you down. You feel like a victim of the rat race. It seems that life is picking up tempo, becoming more rushed, more complicated. Daily hassles seem to be turning into an accepted way of life.

Perhaps you have encountered a mood similar to one from these short scenarios. . . .

BUSY, BUSY, BUSY

It's a typical day at work. Deadlines to meet, phone calls to answer, people's egos and moods to contend with . . . scarcely leaving you a minute of time to unwind as you "grab a bite," scrunched shoulder to shoulder at a busy lunch counter, amidst loud chatter, cigarette smoke and blaring news of gloom and doom from a TV set. To block out the craziness you try to lose yourself in the daily newspaper, but to no avail. Your eyes focus on headlines promising tax hikes and rising unemployment. You're tired of noise, people and their moods, the news and above all, this treadmill race you can't seem to stop. As you stand in line to pay for your undercooked, overpriced lunch, you ask yourself: "Where will it all end?"

HO-HUM BLUES

It's early morning. Your husband has left for another tension-filled day at the office. You are not tense because there is nothing at stake. You do not hold down a "real job," in fact you don't feel like you hold down much of anything. You *do* sort through endless piles of laundry, dirty dishes, and mounds of bed sheets needing to be tucked in place as you make the beds. Your mind tells you that your spirits will lift if you escape for a moment. Ignoring the layer of dust on the television set you switch on a local talk show. The guest is a real dynamite, "with it" person who is doing the kinds of things that you would like to do. You sit in your robe feeling like a "drip." The guest is exciting and a success, and you are telling yourself that you're drab, worn out and stuck in a rut. Exhausted by your self-examination, you either reward yourself with a snack or sneak back under the covers, feeling a bit depressed and confused as to what your role is on this earth.

In each of the two scenes, a hassle, a snag, an external mood of another person caused our "everyman" to experience a *reacting mood*, which was not at all positive. Perhaps you have found yourself automatically reacting to external negatives that have taken their toll on you and brought you down. If that is the case, then you have been a victim of external circumstances.

Worries, doubts, fears that you may feel over everyday hassles can make a strong impression or imprint upon your psychic computer. In the grip of worries, you are being prevented from focusing on anything else. Such negativity marks your energy base with much the same effect as that of a branding iron on a captured beast. Once imprinted with such negativity, you are marked for further negativity.

NIPPING NEGATIVITY IN THE BUD

You cannot avoid going out into the day. Nor can you avoid people.

What you can do, however, is negate or cancel negativity while you are encountering it — be it irritating, negative people, red tape, or trivial hassles.

In getting rid of negativity, you will be using the principle of *thought-energy projection*. Because your projected thought energies shoot electric currents to your point of focus, your projected thoughts can *affect* and *reverse* specific negatives that, up until now, have been ruling your life. By using your psychic mind to project powerful thought energies, you can overcome many obstacles that have stood in your way to success.

There may be times when you are hit head-on with unexpected negativity in your daily encounters, giving you no time to race home, get comfortable and slowly drift to your psychic level. In such situations you will need to take *fast and immediate action*, so as to project a positive mind.

How do you get in touch with your psychic level of mind on such short notice?

Parapsychologists have found that it is possible to reach your psychic level of mind immediately and project instant thought power, just as effectively as if you were at home, seated on a pillow, quietly attaining your psychic level. If you encounter a situation that demands fast and immediate action from your psychic level of mind, do the following three steps:

1 Take in several deep breaths to the count of "In 1 – 2 – 3. . . Out 1 – 2 – 3" (putting you into a more passive state of mind).

2 Mentally say: "I detach!"

3 Mentally say: "White light" (causing your psychic mind to create a shower of white light all around you, preventing any negativity from penetrating your psychic energy base).

Then proceed a step further with any of the following specific exercises to further combat negative forces coming at you. *Please note: the exercises in this book can be tailored by you to fit your specific needs. The affirmations can be paraphrased, if you like. The important thing is that you project your feelings!*

OVERCOMING CERTAIN SPECIFIC NEGATIVE SITUATIONS WITH YOUR PSYCHIC LEVEL OF MIND

First, do the three steps mentioned above. Then, take care of:

ANXIETY

Anxiety can put you in an emotional tailspin, causing you to keep worrying about the same thing, increasing your sense of being a victim as you continue to worry. I remember a client of mine who would be seized by ungrounded fears that something bad was going to happen to her. In tuning into her, I could see clearly that such fears were not psychic, but sheer imagination. Had she been in touch with her psychic mind, she would have been able to *feel* which was which. Needless to say, this woman put herself through needless anguish and a good case of ulcers for nothing.

> When confronted by anxiety, imagine yourself standing in outer space, surrounded by an infinity of divine force. Focus on this idea: There are a billion billion galaxies out there, all around me — around us all. Infinity brings me unlimited peace and happiness. Nothing can interrupt the divine flow of peace, which runs through me at all times!
> Feel the color blue (symbol of outer space) easing over your entire body. Feel cleansed and rid of all turmoil. Feel free of all earth plane anxiety and problems. You are now linked with *infinite force*, which transcends us all. You are *infinite power*!

Using guided imagery or controlled thought projection is a far cry from "loose imagination" that runs away from you. "Getting a handle" on anxiety, through your powerful psychic mind projection, will enable you to be at the controls of your life.

BOREDOM

Not only are you bored, but you feel sluggish and down. You may feel that "nothing is ever going to happen." You need to build an energy momentum or *magnetic force* projected outward that signals to the rest of the world that you are "on a roll." (Everybody loves a winner and is attracted to someone who has things going for him or her.)

> Mentally get in touch with all that you have going for you. If you are feeling at a standstill in the career department, make a mental list (count your blessings) of what good things you have going for you. If you can't find anything in that area of interest, then find another area and feel it spilling over into the area that you

want. Envision a snowball containing images of things already in progress, bringing with it a snowball effect of good things to come.

Mentally say: "Magnetic action spills over into the (select) area of my life. I now have (list wants) happening!"

ERRANDS

Most people get drained just thinking about errands.

I'm one of those people who collapse at the thought of getting in the car, fighting traffic and doing an errand — especially if it is one that doesn't particularly excite me. Do you run any exciting errands? If you don't, then perhaps you will need this next exercise to get through the usual errands:

Imagine a white sail all around your back, as a positive force in back of you. This force is protecting you from getting drained or overtired from the hassles you might encounter. Mentally say three times: "I am sailing through my errands with energy today!"

HABITS

A habit is something programmed to automatically happen regardless of your longings to be free of it. Of course you can always use the garbage can or file system exercises to deprogram yourself. But let's say you are in public and just have to have that cigarette or extra piece of cake because everyone around you is enjoying one or the other. Try this:

Envision the image of the thing that you want to be released from in your psychic mind's eye. See blue light covering it, blocking out its image, so that you are detoxicated of its hold on you. You remain in the blue light, cleansed and soothed.

Mentally say: "The light of peace and health frees me from (name habit)!"

HASSLES

When hassles occur there is no time to run away. You suddenly find yourself wondering "Why me?" In tuning into other people's lives, I do see that the energies around each individual change in frequency with the types of thoughts projected by that individual. Let's take you, for example: If you focus more on the things that you want to happen as opposed to what you fear, you will find things "in general" going smoother for you. You will not have as many hassles to worry about, due to less energy turbulence around you. This, of course, makes way for your radar to project more powerful signals for new positive energy.

The more you practise the various exercises in this book, the more of a feel you will get from being in your psychic level of mind. When hassled:

Mentally envision a white light around you, coming down on you in a shower-like effect. Around that shower is a brick wall, encasing you. The wall is a barrier between you and the hassles of the outside world. Nothing can get in. Mentally focus on the thought that you are encased in positive energy, that all negatives reaching the wall merely bounce off and go away!

HOUSEWORK

This physical labor can be tiring and draining. But if you exercise your psychic level of mind while doing it, you can develop a whole new muscle — a psychic computer — that will project signals that you are magnetic and that you attract the very best of everything.

There is something exhilarating about projecting your mind energies while doing a physical exercise. If you think about it, you are actually doubling your forces. I have done this next exercise often. Not only have I experienced successes in the days to follow, but I have a shinier floor. At first, you may feel a bit silly. I sure did! But just apply some more "elbow grease" to the exercise and you'll get the feel of it.

And remember: there is no such thing as silly to your computer, which believes everything that you feed it!

When you image and project thought energies with your psychic mind, you can increase your impact by combining physical action with focus, forming *total force*. When you are faced with house-hold tasks, consider imaging the following as you do them:

Mopping: "I cleanse my house and my life with old energies."

Windows: "Positive energies now shine into my life."

Sink:　　　"Release all worries down the drain."

Dusting:　　"I wipe away all negativity from my life."

Arranging:　"There is a divine order to my life."

NEWS OF THE DAY

I see so many people on the streets who walk with a weighed down air. In "connecting" with them, I see that they are among those who believe all the news about inflation, hard times, world crises, crime. I'm not saying that those things do not exist. What I am saying is that sometimes I observe news "in-any-way-made-commercial" containing hype along with the facts. I respect the news stations and papers that bring us the news. But do remember: These commercial news channels are wording stories, no matter how factual, in a way designed to arrest and grab your attention. And the fact that the news places emphasis on struggle, strife, tension, and uncertainty means the reinforcement of the image: times are tough!

It would be foolish to avoid the news, since it is the news that makes you aware of happenings that could affect you. Equally foolish would be to harbor fears and thoughts centered around the "Times Are Tough" image. You can avoid being drained and manipulated by unnecessary hysteria in the air:

The next time you hear or read the news, mentally envision yourself in a bubble of white light. Mentally say: "I am a part of all that is positive and good. Negative news does not affect me."

FOOD FIXATION

You seem to be functioning from one feeding to another. The only satisfaction you seem to be getting these days is food. It is the only thing that keeps you going. Eating gives you a sense of enjoyment, a sense of reward and a sense of love. The amount of emotion you pour into food is programming your computer to live to eat. You find yourself at a low ebb and listless without your "food fix."

You need to deprogram yourself. You can do the garbage can or filing exercise. But if you haven't got the time and that caloric source of love is staring you in the face . . . what do you do? Here's what has worked for many, including myself, a reformed "chocoholic."

(Warning: This exercise might offend your sense of taste . . . .)
Mentally feel yourself to be shooting the food with a gun that
ejects maggots. Imagine your food target to be oozing with maggots. Mentally say to yourself: "(The food) is a dead issue with
me. I have no use for it in my life!"

To reinforce and program your psychic computer carry a few
3 × 5 cards with a statement such as: "Snacking is a dead issue; I
have no use for it in my life!"

PEOPLE

Annoying People

Someone around you is driving you crazy! Not only is he distracting
you, but he is putting you under stress.

I think immediately of restaurants, with loud people occupying
the next table. If they make loud, smacking noises while eating, I
immediately start this next exercise. Not only has it saved my sanity,
I might add, but it has prevented me from swinging on the nearest
chandelier out of frustration. But more important — this exercise
cuts and destroys any negativity that would have built up within
you.

When annoyed by people, the first thing that you need to do is
to break their spell over you. These people have taken your time and
your energies; you have been captured by their signals. You need to
send forth your own powerful signals:

Envision a white shield coming down around the person who is
the source of the irritation. Then envision a white shield around
yourself, locking out all irritation. Know that both you and the
person are separate from the noise or trouble that he has been
stirring up. If you can, picture an exaggerated symbol of the
irritation itself, outside of you and the person. If the source of
irritation is gum chewing, then mentally picture its symbol —
such as a wad of gum, or lips smacking gum. Know that this silly
irritant is on the outside, having no relationship to you and to
the person who initiated it. Mentally say: "I am shielded from
all irritations!"

Bill Collectors

"They make me feel so poor!" complained one woman. Another said that bill collectors took her back to the days when she had done something "naughty" as a little girl. Perhaps you have encountered creditors. If you do in the future, remember: you need to get across the message — "Back off! I'm a good person!" Your psychic radar can project such powerful forces on your behalf.

Concentrate on this thought — we all have a divine self or higher spirit that is God-like and operates on a high plane, responding to the goodness in us that we project. The goodness in you can reach the goodness in another, no matter how he or she is treating you, by simply making a psychic connection between your level of goodness and *theirs*.

Mentally envision that person (the bill collector) having an "angel self" around him. While he or she is giving you a hard time on the physical plane, connect with the powerful energy plane by reaching him psychically with this thought going over and over in your mind: "To the angel self of (bill collector) I connect with your divine goodness! Only good comes from this encounter!"

Draining People

Have you ever been in the company of someone, when — after a few minutes — you begin to sag and feel like the life has just gone out of you? I recall talking on the phone to such a lady once: after a few minutes, I was so drained that I felt slightly depressed. I should have said goodbye and hung up. But no — I fell asleep! (I don't think she knew the difference, because when I awoke, she was still talking a mile a minute!)

Should you find yourself with someone who drains your energies, remember: Even though the person is robbing you of your vitality for the moment, he is not necessarily a negative person. It simply means that he is getting "a battery charge" from your energies, without giving you a "boost" in return.

To prevent energy loss: Merely cross your legs and arms. (Of course, if you are standing, this might create a problem, to say nothing of a spectacle.) If standing, cross just your arms. Mentally envision a white glow around yourself and around the other person. Mentally say: *"Vital energy!"* At the same time, focus on the glow growing brighter and brighter as you repeat the statement.

I do the above exercise on planes, buses, subways, in the middle of a lecture if I feel the crowd feeding off of my energy. It's sort of like a vitamin B.12 shot to the mind.

Manipulative People

Whoever is manipulating you has a psychic feeling that he is reaching you and causing you to do what *he* wants you to do. The manipulator, like the spider catching a fly, knows that he has *caught* you in his web.

You must transmit psychic signals that mean you are not trapped by anyone! That person does not have any power over you!

> To stop manipulation: Look between the manipulator's eyes. This breaks the psychic hold, as most manipulation takes place with suggestive eye contact. Next, envision a spider's web oozing out from that *chakra* and entangling the person in a web of his own manipulative energy. This does not harm the person at all. It merely stops his power over you.

This is a great exercise for anyone who feels "dangled," "strung along," or "held in bondage" by anybody.

Obnoxious People

You are being hit with billions of bolts of energy — negative energy thrust at you by obnoxious people. Your computer is recording the fact that you are a victim. You need to stop the attack immediately!

Wouldn't it be nice if there were a cosmic white light spray gun that you could have on hand with which to handle obnoxious people? Perhaps the following exercise is the next best thing.

> Mentally focus upon a white light with a mirror surrounding it, going outward. All negativity bounces off the reflection, returning to its source (or disappearing in the light — if you prefer). Mentally say: "Negativity to negativity." (Or, "Negativity disappears into the light.")

This exercise not only gives you a power boost, but gets the signals across to the opponent that you are too powerful to be stepped on!

Waiting on People

And I don't mean waiting tables. Business matters will be found in Chapter Six. What I am speaking about is that god-awful feeling of "waiting around" for someone to make up his mind or come to a decision on a matter related to you. While waiting, you start to feel at the mercy of the other party. You don't feel in control. In fact, the more you wait, the more you feel like a puppet! In reality, perhaps we are all puppets — but not to each other. Rather, we are puppets to something greater than ourselves that can move us into positive new spaces, provided we are *in touch*. The next time you are made to feel like someone's puppet, focus on the fact that there is a power — perhaps a divine one — to which we are *all* connected. And that person who has you on the string is connected to a higher force — something that you can tap into, moving you *above* the limitations of this one individual.

This next exercise puts you in touch with greater powers. It removes you from the role of victim and places you in the driver's seat of your own emotions and moods. Many have found that doing this exercise helps speed things up and the person they were waiting on suddenly comes around!

When waiting: Image and focus upon a gigantic ball of light. Rays shoot from it, linking it directly to you. See the ball of light start to roll ahead, pulling you with it. See this ball of light reaching the person (who has kept you waiting), and moving right *through* him in a transparent glow. See it pulling you right through that person, while you image yourself to be a white, transparent glow. Notice how good it feels to be light and free of the weight that this person has put upon your shoulders! You are white-light goodness. You are divine energy. No one can keep you from your goal! Know this! See the person, magnetized to your light, start to follow you!

This can really work wonders, so hang onto your hat!

RED TAPE

Red tape is not my idea of a good time. But I do have fun with this next exercise, because it not only relaxes me in the face of red tape, it creates energies that affect the general day, red tape included. This is a potent exercise to try.

When face to face with red tape or in a situation where you are trying to maintain your individual power and rights while confronted by The System, do this:

> Feel yourself in a soft green light . . . separated from the hassles of red tape. Cooled. Calmed down from any hysteria that red tape created. Whatever person (or thing) is causing this red tape, feel and see a funnel of soft green light go around him also. This helps create an air about that person that is calm, enabling him to process your cause with ease. Green rays, according to Kirlian research, are extremely relaxing and soothing to the nerves. Know that all is well.

After typing this exercise in the original manuscript, I got so relaxed, I had to take a nap, letting the red tape of correcting errors bathe in the green light!

TRAFFIC

You are caught in traffic. Exhaust fumes, noise, and cars — bumper to bumper — are invading your space and peace of mind.

It all looks so primitive to me at times — the sight of these separate rolling contraptions all headed in one direction. In the meantime, primitive or not, these rolling contraptions need not get to you — and their drivers as well. Traffic stress can affect your business day, your hours at home, and your social life. When confronted with the hassles of traffic, you need to detach yourself from the craziness and tension inflicted upon you:

> Mentally envision your car to be in a bubble of white light. Focus upon the image that your energy is contained and protected as you roll in this bubble, carrying you to your destination full of peace, energy and magnetism.

TRAUMA

You are panicked! If you have ever encounterd trauma, you might recall that gut-level panic that probably occurred. When I am tuning into a person who is in a state of trauma, I can feel that person's energies putting him in a tailspin effect — with turbulence creating more trauma, and increased trauma creating more turbulence! Such an effect of "being sucked into a funnel of negativity" can go on for days, even weeks if you let it.

This exercise is one that can release you from the trauma that has kept you in turmoil:

> Mentally envision a shield of tinted glass coming between you and the traumatic event, or person or thing that caused you the trauma. See and feel the shield giving off a cooling sensation, with a vapor effect, reaching and cleaning out your psychic energy base and the very depths of your body. Your body is calmed and soothed. Mentally say: "I am cool, I am calm, I am separated from trauma!"

WEATHER

At times we react negatively to the first signs of bad weather. Regardless of whether the forecast follows through, we find things falling apart around us. Why? Because your computer is obeying your frantic call of "Bad storm ahead — nothing will go right!"

At the first sign of bad weather, merely program yourself for good things instead:

> Image the sun shining overhead and sending out brilliant rays of light all around you. You can go one step further and envision actual scenes of events and things that you would like to see happen in your life. Just picture them on the gold rays shooting down at you.

> Mentally say: "My life is rays of happiness! I give thanks for (list goals, aims — both large-scale and immediate for the day)."

This exercise prevents you from being "psyched out" by ominous weather reports that dictate the moods, the activities and the accomplishments of people the world over. Doing this exercise will end your being a victim to the forces of nature.

UNCERTAINTIES

The tension of uncertainties can cause your psychic radar to signal others that you are a victim of waiting and wondering "what will happen to little me?"

Many people approach me for professional guidance as to the possibilities that lie ahead. Those who want to know if I can see the dates, the times, the events that are for certain going to happen are bid a fast: "Sorry — go to Madam Zeena down at the pier. She has a great crystal ball and will tell you any date that you want to hear." Some people have left my place in a huff upon hearing this: after all, I'm a professional psychic, I should see everything!

"I'm not God, honey — I only work for 'im!" snapped a tired fortune-teller once to a friend of mine.

It seems that many of us would like to get an edge on the future by simply tuning into its many possibilities, which are all around us. And the more psychically in tune you become through practice, the more you will find that such matters as dates and times are next to impossible to nail down. Why? Because, one's future, whose energy possibilities already exist, contains many options that one can "pull in" — based on one's attitudes, emotions, and state of mind at the time.

I suppose that many of us could go round and round debating and wondering which exists — free will or destiny. In my counselings, as I look in on a person's future options, I often see a combination of both — where some options are attached to such strong energy that they are *bound* to happen. This is perhaps a form of destiny. Sometimes upon looking in on someone's energies, I perceive that some future possibilities are coming to him if only he were to *focus* upon them. I don't have a pat answer to this, but I do see both kinds of energies prevalent in many people.

In the meantime, if you are uncertain about either your present condition or your future, there is an exercise that can relieve you of stress caused by such a limbo state. Not only will the energies from the exercise make you feel more in control, but those same electromagnetic energies will be reaching the outside world with your signals that you are on the right path. (*You are a success.* And everybody loves a winner, so be ready for sudden, improved changes in the uncertainty area.)

As for knowing what lies ahead for you, the last chapter will get into that. Now let's tackle your uncertainties:

Mentally say: "My life has a divine pattern to it. I am taking the right steps! The right path is cleared for me!"

The exercise by itself will calm you. In time, it will allow you to start getting feelings about directions to take.

UNEMPLOYMENT

The best thing you could do to resolve this is the garbage can or file exercise. Another way to program your computer is by means of a 3 × 5 card taped to your bathroom mirror. In the morning and at night, while grooming yourself, read what is on the card: "I am prepared for and will attract the right job!"

Both my husband and I use the 3 × 5 card method to attract the jobs and creative assignments that we want. I sometimes carry cards in my purse to glance at throughout the day. In no time at all, new events and opportunities come on in!

FEARS — A SECTION OF ITS OWN

If you have ever been scared about anything or anybody, you will know the crippling effect that fear has. Not only do you feel exposed to forces beyond your control, but you feel powerless in the face of them. Below are some specific situations to help you take care of your fear:

WHILE ALONE

You are alone in the house. You think you hear a noise. After taking precautionary measures for your safety, you still feel uneasy — perhaps even frightened. To reverse those unwarranted fears:

> Close your eyes and mentally call upon the white light to surround you in a bonfire fashion. See and focus upon the image of it rising up to infinity where there is a *divine creator who is linked up to you and your safety.* (If divine creator does not fit with your beliefs, then focus on *infinite good forces* that are hooking up with you.) Mentally say: *"Protection!"*

Next, on a sheet of paper, make a list of goals, hopes and even dreams that you would like to see happen in your life. They can be in the same column. Some people like to go a step further and create two columns — one for long-range goals, and one for short, immediate goals and wishes. Then on the back of that paper list the things that you now have to be thankful for — no matter how small.

Go back to the "goals side" of the paper, and one by one go through the goals and take a moment with each — envisioning how it would feel to have it fulfilled. Take a moment and "live" the feelings you would feel if the goal you are focusing on were to come into your life.

When you have finished, mentally say: "All is well!" — and feel it!

By first listing your goals, you are breaking the hold that fear has had upon you. You are correcting the negative data entered into your computer, by installing its *positive replacement*. By listing a few things that you have to be thankful for you are reinforcing your computer with the data that you are in a good and deserving state for more good things to come your way! With such data, now go to the goal list again and with increased positive energies, signal one and all that all is well.

I have used this exercise countless times when I was traveling alone through strange cities. Not only were my fears arrested, but I generated enough positive signals to pull in exciting new things in the days ahead.

PHOBIAS

Though each phobia is different from the next, there seems to be a similarity insofar as each phobia is a chronic occurrence that takes hold of one repeatedly in some situations. To break the hold that a phobia might have on you:

> Envision a hand with a white light around it holding yours. Mentally say: "I am at one with the divine hand of a loving force (or God) that is now guiding me away from fear. I am free of all fears."

HOW POSITIVE PSYCHIC COMMUNICATION IS YOUR BEST WEAPON AGAINST NEGATIVITY FROM OTHERS

Love is a binding force. So is anger. The difference between the two is that love's bond enables both parties to thrive on positive things, to grow, to blossom with vital energy each day. If there are spats or fights, once the air is cleared that "loving air" enables the partners to enrich their lives once more. Anger, on the other hand, is a ball-and-chain force that clamps down upon the initiator, not the target. Not being a true psychic or positive force, it creates turbulence in the air — mainly for the one who creates the anger. I once met a woman who was so full of anger towards her ex-husband that she was literally crippled with arthritic pain. She also suffered from headaches, stomach disorders, and deep depressions that would go on for days. Her ex-husband, however, had remarried and made a new life for himself. He wished his ex well, and never failed to send her more than what was due in alimony. He was radiant, in excellent health, and was encountering new strokes of good luck continually. He was not bound to the woman simply because he wished her well. Even though the marriage was over, he still sent her a form of love and was therefore "in the light" as far as energies go. With such positive energies signaling "good vibes," the man was forever attracting positive things into his life. The woman, however, by harboring hatred and anger, locked up her chances for any new successes. Because she was in darkness, her life was bound to dark and gloomy events.

Psychologists will be the first to tell you that anger is healthy *if* it is expressed in some way, then released. I have noticed many a person holding onto a grudge over the years — attracting to them series of "bad things." Holding a grudge only holds you to the dark energy of unexpressed anger; you keep negativity within you.

"I'm mad at my mother-in-law!" spouted one man at the seminar. "Can I be excused to go throw darts at her?"

No doubt this is what the man wanted to do! But of course such action, being negative, would have hurt him because he had inflicted pain on another; and those directed negative forces of his would have "boomeranged" on him. Suffice it to say that such anger would be best taken out jogging around the block, working out at the gym, or even in doing something creative. I know of one woman who, when riled by her in-laws, takes it out on her petunia bed — creating a beautiful garden for herself.

The next time you are attacked by someone's negativity, know that that very negativity is indeed heading back to them as they project it. But so that you don't have to be drained or feel the tensions of their negativity, your best defense is to project positive energies through your psychic mind. The next time someone gives you a face-to-face problem in public, your best defense is any of the on-the-spot exercises from any of these chapters. Projecting positive psychic energies in the face of negativity can turn you into an impenetrable fortress through which no negatives can enter. Being "in the light" in the face of negativity makes it impossible for anyone's anger to grip you.

"What if you're thinking negatively when all along you thought you were thinking positively?" asked a concerned woman.

"Once you start using your psychic level of mind," I told her, "you will begin to get a 'feel' for whether you are in harmony with positive mental focus."

Practising psychic projection creates within you a strong inner awareness of "where you're at" with respect to positives and negatives. It is just something that you know after a time, just as you get a feel for a town or a living place after a while.

DEFENSE AGAINST NEGATIVE ANGER DIRECTED TOWARD YOU

Image yourself as a giant magnet with iron filing rays of white shooting out from every inch of your body. These rays are positive energy, and are hitting and affecting others, including the source of negativity aimed at you.

You are now a radiating positive magnet that knows only "good." Such focus prepares you to face the day with more power and light — your best offense against attack.

A WORD ABOUT PSYCHIC ATTACK

The phrase *psychic attack* connotes black magic, voodoo, and evil spells. These things exist, of course, but are not what most people think they are. This "power" is derived from *scaring* the target, or by planting within one the *fear* of the evil spell coming true — thus imprinting one's computer with data that reads: I am a victim. One starts to believe that one is a victim of that spell, and soon subconsciously finds oneself living out the fate of what one was told would happen. Such power over another person is negative or "evil," as some would call it. But one basic truth underlies it all — that the person receiving the spell is programmed by the verbal power of suggestion to be his *own* destructor. You might say that in such a situation, a person's computer is programmed to self-destruct.

"Do you have to know if you are under psychic attack for it to work?" asked three paranoid voices in unison.

"Yes — boo!" I replied.

I went on: "Because we all have inner feelings of how others regard us, we can't help but be aware of their attacks on us, if, say, they were to let us know in some way that they intended us harm."

"Could they let you know mentally?" asked one lady who was growing uneasy.

"Psychically? Yes, because we all have radar systems. Let's say that your sister in Timbuctu is mad at you. Let's say that she wants to cause you harm . . . ."

"Could she?" interrupted the same voice.

"No. Don't forget that she is sending forth negative energy. It is therefore not a psychic energy and it — being a negative force — is already boomeranging back upon her!" I replied.

"So she can't cause any harm to me or to my family!" the woman sighed with relief.

"Rest assured, no one can cause you to do anything against your will. No one can cause you pain. No one can cause you harm," I said.

What happens when some people are "under the spell" of a witch, for example, is that they mentally "pick up" the fact that negative energy is directed their way. What they don't see is that such negative energy is *not* reaching them. What *is* reaching them is the feeling — and just a feeling — that someone wishes them ill. Now, if they were to take this worry for what it is and *forget it* — or better yet, do an exercise for it — they would be in great shape. Instead, their fear and imagination run away with them, creating such thoughts as "I am meant to suffer," "I am doomed," and their computers pick up the data and "run" with it.

Developing your psychic mind power to the fullest extent can enhance your awareness of just how powerful you are in the face of any destructive forces, which can't hurt you if you don't accept them!

Have you ever entered a room — only to be hit in the face with jealousy and general negative vibes? I would suggest this next exercise. This one is great for job applicants who have to sit together in the same waiting room. I have used it successfully at cocktail parties, which often abound with such forces. If you are confronted with general jealousies in a group situation, keep in mind that those jealousies may not be those of people wishing you ill. It may be merely their own frail insecure energies surfacing as they eye you. Still, you want to be free of their tension, so that you can be your own person:

IF JEALOUSIES HIT YOU IN THE FACE

Envision yourself covered in a clear plastic see-through bubble, where all "bad vibes" merely roll off your back. No negativity can invade your psychic energy base. Envision yourself carrying a flashlight, like a positive beam projected outward, attracting the right people to you. Now you can relax and know that you don't have to write off any function as totally negative. There might be some warm and friendly people out there in the midst of the rotten ones. Mentally say: "I attract the highest and best to me."

As you become increasingly aware that negativity can be negated, replaced by positive force, you will become more comfortable using these positive forces in your daily life. And with such comfort replacing anxiety, you can't help but be programmed for positive, successful results.

Let's take a look now at your personal life and how to make some dynamic changes for the better!

5

Improving Your Home and Personal Life

When the phrase *personal life* is mentioned, most people conjure up images of hot, heavy romantic scenes. And if romance is what you are seeking, this chapter has an entire section just for those needs. In the meantime, you exist with your other personal needs, emotions and concerns. You are your personal life. You may go to work in the morning and put in more than a full day of work. At quitting time you are left with yourself and those personal needs of yours. You proceed with whatever personal life you have made for yourself — be it going home to a family, to an empty apartment, or not going home at all. Even if you go the workaholic route, working through the night, you are fulfilling needs that personally belong to you at that moment, in this case — work. Your personal needs and your personal life follow you everywhere. If you care to introduce some romance into them, that is up to you. You are the "radar base" for anything or anybody you would like to draw into your life. You can make things happen by using your powerful psychic signals.

I have found that those who cultivate and gain a satisfying personal life — with or without romance — are the ones who have a solid home base from which to launch projects in the career or financial aspects of their lives. As the personal area of your life is directly related to you, it is only natural that as you improve it, so do you improve your self-image. A better self-image sends stronger signals to the world: you deserve to be a success.

I knew a woman who was overweight due to chronic overeating. She was unhappy with herself, putting her self-image on a low scale. Her signals to her fellow workers at a radio station were: "I'm a slob" — "I'm a nobody." In my visits to the radio station, I was appalled at the way her fellow workers treated this seemingly intelligent, warm lady. To be frank about it — they treated her like a worthless clump of dirt. Although she had the expertise and experience to be promoted, she was passed over continually, as the managers chose some "cute," outspoken neophyte who was less intelligent. Her luck did not change until she started liking herself. In her case, liking herself meant losing weight. Such a change of appearance meant a whole new set of "signals" sent to the managers: "I'm valuable!" The last time I heard, she was an associate producer of a highly popular program.

I have always done much better in life if I felt good about myself, inside and out. I have also noticed that if anything were happening for the "bad" at home, I would carry it with me, even if it was in the back of my mind, into work that day. I have also noticed that when things ran smoothly for me, with my personal needs met, that air of success would spill over with great impact into my work — creating success after success in all areas of my life.

To get some positive things going for you, to make positive events happen, you must start with you and the image that you carry of yourself within your computer. If you have been working with a negatively programmed self-image, then you are sure to be pulling in less than positive circumstances for yourself. If you took the precautions in Chapter Three and dumped your negative self-image in the garbage, you might be asking yourself: "Where do I go from here? How do I create a more positive self-image?"

To be a positive, magnetic person, you must live the part! "Become that which you want to be," as a famous philosopher once said. Every once in a while I meet someone who, in private, can't stand the sight of himself, but in public will momentarily put on a front for the occasion. That approach to positive thinking does not work. It, like foundation makeup, is surface and is a front, not the real thing. What you want to start doing is creating an air that will stay with you despite the occasion.

THAT CERTAIN AIR

Have you ever been in a restaurant where everyone was dressed to the hilt when a man walked dressed in jeans, a faded shirt and worn-out loafers with no socks? You glance at him. Something tells you that money just walked through the door. From the way the staff treats him, it is evident that he is somebody important, confirming your initial gut reaction. He had a certain air about him that signaled "money" to you and to others in the restaurant. That certain air was, of course, his self-image, transmitted from his psychic energy base. In his mind, he was first-class in appearance, first-class in talk, first-class in carriage. He knew that he had a first-class bank account, thanks to his first-class job.

I mentioned this scenario to a group of unemployed women who were meeting weekly for therapy. One of them reacted: "Well, he had plenty to be positive about. I'd feel first-class if I had a first-class job and bank account, too."

Agreed. It is easy to project positive psychic signals to the world when you are on top of the world. But the main point is this: The man was a complete stranger to the people in the restaurant. He was less well-dressed than the others who were dining there. Yet, that air that he was projecting automatically forced everyone to take note. Here is someone special!

"What about us peons who have to work for a living?" asked one lady. "Can we project an air of glamour and magnetism despite the fact that we have to take so much from haughty customers?"

My answer was a big yes. "You can project anything you set your mind on," I told her.

If you program your computer with "first-class" images about yourself, you will be setting yourself up for first-class reactions from the world around you.

"Can't you be setting yourself up for disappointment?" asked a cautious man who had seen his share of disappointments. "What if you really *are* bad news, but start convincing yourself that you are hot potatoes?"

"Who are you really?" was my reaction. "You are the physical and mental extension of your own computer!"

In other words, you are the sum total of your thoughts and feelings that you have had about yourself. You are your self-image. Let's say that you are an athlete who wants to pursue an active professional life of sports. If you were to use your psychic level of mind to focus on yourself as Olympic material, it would not at all be a false thing to do. You would be creating Olympic-type energies that would help you send strong success signals to the world, whether you eventually got to the Olympics or not. I have seen many a person "pull into" his life, though, the same equivalents of what they were dwelling on with their psychic minds.

By changing your self-image, you will be changing all that you pull into your life. In focusing on the image of the person that you want to become, you are in no way lying to yourself. You are stretching the truth of who you are *now* to become who you know you *can* be.

You may not have a first-class bank account or a first-class image of yourself, yet you can activate your psychic level of mind to start signaling to the world that you are a success. As your magnetism builds, you are likely to feel better about who you are, resulting in an increase of positive people and events in your life.

CREATING A DYNAMIC NEW YOU

Take a few moments and decide in your mind what things or aspects about yourself you would like to improve on. It sometimes helps to get the aspects firmly set in your mind by jotting them down. (No more than five, so as not to overload.) The mere fact that you have put them on paper helps your computer lock into the data all the more, even though you need not read the list while doing the exercise.

STEPS TO CREATING A DYNAMIC NEW YOU

The Steps:

1 Close your eyes and feel yourself showered in a white light that is pulling you down, down a long, slippery slide. As you slide downward, feel the light, relaxed feeling as you shed yourself of all worries, doubts, and negativity.

2 When you feel you have reached the bottom of the slide, find yourself in your own private room. Get into your overstuffed white easy chair. Get comfortable, feeling your body fall limp.

3 In front of you envision your work table, where "you make things happen."

4 On that table create an image of you, the way you want to be. Especially at first, you may not always be able to actually see yourself with your inner mind. If you can't, it simply means that you are not used to doing the exercise — nothing more. By merely commanding your computer to envision that image, you are, however, creating that very reality on the energy plane and that is what counts. Over a period of time, with practice, you will begin to see better and more clearly. In the meantime, don't worry. Not seeing any image has no affect on the outcome.

5 Have in mind the things about yourself that you want to improve upon.

6 Take a few moments and feel yourself climbing into your image that is on the work table.

7 While inside that image command yourself to feel and experience the positive feelings you would feel if this new image were to be yours right now.

8 Take this a step further and feel yourself as the new you who is relating to and attracting good feelings from the people who know you. Feel you-the-new-image encountering success with strangers. Actually live the part. The more emotion you can put into this exercise, the greater your successes will be!

9 When you have had enough, mentally put a white light around yourself as a boost (mentally say: "White light!"), and count yourself back to wide-awake level with a 1–2–3.

It would be easy to think beautiful thoughts if it weren't for "so danged many people!" complained a disgruntled complaints clerk. Perhaps you have had this same feeling at one time.

I have found that it is indeed possible to create a momentum of good energies that can follow you through your day, allowing you to maintain your own power in the face of whatever it is that happens to you.

The fourth chapter showed you some fast and effective exercises to do on the spot, when confronted by "specifics." This next exercise is one that you do in the privacy of your home, even before you get out of bed in the morning. Doing it is like taking out some energy insurance to further insure you of a good day ahead.

SOME INSURANCE FOR A GOOD DAY AHEAD

The Steps:

1 Close your eyes and command yourself to be sliding very gently down a smooth, slippery slide. You are a dreamy white cloud, feeling wonderful and at peace. You are bigger than life!

2 As a bigger-than-life cloud, you walk through your town, bouncing lightly over the rooftops and the trees. You are free from the pull of trivial matters. You are strong. (Don't call yourself big because that might program you to gain weight! Bigger-than-life is okay because that is a symbol image.)

3 Take a moment and go into certain scenes that you might be encountering, such as your work scene, or social scenes, errand scenes, and so forth — all the while being an image of bigger-than-it-all. (Such an image programs your computer for you to be big and strong, and above and beyond all small, petty things that could get you down. This exercise, which is *divine programming*, will not make you feel superior or uppity to anyone.)

4 When you are ready to come back to external reality, mentally count: "1–2–3 wide awake."

The above exercise programs your computer to prepare you for a better day than you would usually have, and it sends forth signals to the world that you are on top of things.

From my experience with clients, I have discovered two traps that can create havoc with your personal life, if you fall prey to them.

TRAP #1: THE STAMP OF APPROVAL TRAP

To be avoided at all costs! Why? Because when you fall victim to needing someone's approval in any daily situation, you program your computer to create you as "less-than" the person you are trying to please. That person's computer receives your psychic signals, loud and clear, and causes him to automatically behave as if he were superior to you. If you are the least bit insecure, you feel all the more need to get this person's approval, and you therefore send out more intense messages to him that you are beneath him, that you are striving to measure up to him. Take note of a critical point here: the fact that your computer is signaling to him that "I am struggling!" creates the reality of you struggling for approval, without an end to it. You risk riding a vicious merry-go-round of programming yourself for an inferior image, and then sending forth negativity that says to others as well: "I am a nothing, you can dump on me and I'll struggle to please you."

TAKING EFFECTIVE ACTION

I have seen many a client appear bound to others, simply because he was dedicated to pleasing.

I went through a phase several years back where I felt I had to gain everybody's approval before I could feel important. Not only was I miserable all the time, because it was impossible to please everybody, but I was also in a position of weakness because I gave so much power to other people over myself.

ENDING THE-NEED-TO-PLEASE

When caught with the urge to seek the approval of others, envision yourself covered with a dazzling shower of white diamonds. Focus the image of your being as sparkling, radiant and magnetic. Mentally say: "I do not need the approval of others. I am aglow with divine power."

TRAP #2: THE LET-ME-IMPRESS-YOU TRAP

It is easy to be pulled into another's script where he or she is playing a role and coerces you to take part in the scene. Let's say that you are at the hairdresser's, surrounded by women who have the need to impress everyone with their money and position in the community. Their discussion not only makes you feel less than them, but it also makes you feel like a real "nothing" if you sit there like a lump and aren't part of the in-group. A fluttery feeling erupts in your stomach; you feel a pressure urging you to let them know that, "I am worth something, too!" What do you do?

I bring up this scenario because I was an eyewitness to a similar event one day, while at a chic hair salon in Beverly Hills. I sat and observed three women trying to outclass each other. It went something like this:

First woman: "I've been invited to a star-studded party tonight. Anyone who is *anyone* will be there! But I left my *five*-hundred-dollar dress at my condo in Palm Springs."

Second woman: "Had you notified me last night, dear, I could have spent the morning walking through my closets, picking a designer original you could have squeezed into."

Third woman: "I'm sure she doesn't want to wear last year's designs, dear. By the way (to first woman), I noticed a cute little dress down the street for only eight hundred dollars . . . on sale."

First woman: "Well, actually, I was planning on paying a limo to pick up my dress and drive it to the city for tonight."

Second woman: "Why *pay* for a limo, when you can use one of ours? We have three, after all . . . ."

And so on . . . with the conversation getting more and more exaggerated, and the participants falling into an abyss of their own negative jealousies.

ENDING THE NEED TO IMPRESS

If you feel the urge coming over you to impress people around you, take heed and do the following short exercise; it will stop this destructive urge, dead in its tracks.

Mentally envision and feel a glorious white crown on your head, with rays shooting out from it in all directions. Focus on the thought that you are a child of supreme, radiant energy! (Or a Supreme Creator.) Know that as you focus on this thought, others will be impressed with the fact that you are your own source of power. You are not dependent on others!

I have seen various insecure people use this exercise and thereby overcome old inhibitions and fears, while gaining new self-respect and a sense of power.

THE NITTY-GRITTY OF RELATIONSHIPS

Now to the fun part!

If you are like most people, you will probably want to skip the preceding stuff and concentrate on the section that shows you how to pull in that man or woman of your dreams. Fine — knowing what you want is half the battle, as they say. But if you go into battle without a strong armor or self-image, you are likely to lose.

What comes to mind is the scene of a person gorging on junk foods, yet daydreaming of the day when his body will be in terrific shape. That day, of course, never comes, simply because he has not put in time preparing for it — he has not even begun to cut out the junk foods and replace them with nutritious fare.

By wanting to better your personal life, you are setting up a goal, just as the "junk-food junkie" should set a goal. In your case you can achieve your goal by doing some strong mental groundwork with your psychic mind. Feed your computer healthy and positive images and it will build a healthy and positive life for you. Feed it "junk," or negatives, and you will be like the junk-food junkie — still waiting for the better life to come.

IF YOU ARE SINGLE AND LOOKING

It is hard to find that right person, especially if you try to physically track him (or her) down. I know of many people who have used such strategies as barhopping, dance-hall combing, even grocery shopping to find someone who might be right for them. Many connected and many found that that Mr. Right or Ms Perfect were *not* right at all.

So where do you start to find that perfect love partner?

I remember doing a TV talk show where viewers called in for "psychic advice." One lady with a distinct whine to her voice asked me "how her chances were" for finding a man. On tuning into her energies I could feel that she was radiating the right signals to pull one in. (She was a magnetic lady who was right for that sort of involvement.) A month passed, and I was doing another live call-in advice on that same Los Angeles TV station. As I took the next call, I heard a familiar whining voice: " ... So where *is* he?" Had she done anything to meet someone? (And I didn't mean barhop.) I meant simply had she ventured forth into new social situations? As it turned out the woman had never left her apartment! (Can you imagine a scenario where she is sitting at home waiting for Mr. Perfect to ring her doorbell? I made it clear to her that in order to meet someone she might have to leave the confines of home!)

What if you are in love or attracted to someone, but the target of your interest is not responding. What do you do?

First, don't panic. And above all, do not think of yourself as failing or you'll have to resort to "dumping some more garbage" again. This next exercise will hook you up with the target of your affection. And while connected to him (or her), you will also get a feeling as to whether or not this person is the right person for you.

HOOKING UP TO THE TARGET OF YOUR AFFECTIONS

The Steps:

1 Go to your psychic level of mind by one of the previous methods used thus far in the book.

2 Climb into your white overstuffed easy chair and get comfortable.

3 On your work table envision the image of the person to whom you are attracted. Command your mind to create the image of him or her in as much detail as possible. (Even though you may not be able to "see" all of it, your computer is creating the reality on the energy planes by sending forth signals of your being in touch with that person.)

4 See a picture of yourself standing next to your love interest.

5 Climb into your body and feel the sensations you would feel if the two of you were involved in a happy, healthy relationship. Feel yourself holding hands with this person, and feel your energies connecting.

6 While connected mentally feel yourself telling this person all of your good points — reasons that the two of you would "go well" together. Feel the person smiling as you talk. Feel it all taking place. You are a happy couple!

7 When finished count back to conscious level in 1–2–3.

By actually taking a few moments each morning and evening — twice a day — for as long as you want, you can start to make things happen in your personal life. The key is to really live the role while you are doing the exercise. That way, you are imprinting your computer with heavy data that read: *I am happily involved with you* to the "target."

"What if that target doesn't want to have anything to do with me?" asked a heartbroken woman.

"Then you'll get the feeling soon enough that that very person is not at all right for you. It is a general gut feeling that you get, which is a form of psychic ability," I responded. I advised the woman, in such a case, to simply envision a white glowing light on the table — a symbol for the right energies of the right person for *her*, to be pulled into her life.

How can this happen, you might ask.

Remember, your radar system is sending and receiving signals, involving you with a network of connected energies out there. When you send forth an energy signal that says: I now have the right person for me — the right person out there "picks up" the signal in an automatic subconscious manner and comes into the picture, though he consciously may not know that it was a signal that brought him in. The total network of everybody else's energies all around you is called *the collective unconscious* by psychologists. Suffice to know that you, a radar, are hooked up with the right person already. It is simply a matter of sending the right signal.

I tried the above exercise of imagining a white light with myself standing next to it, holding his hand. The very next day I met my future husband!

THE AFFAIR

If you are trying to "hook up" with someone who is already involved, you may find it extremely difficult to connect with this person, especially if he or she is happily married. The marital bond is a positive bond that truly connects man and wife on the physical, spiritual and emotional planes. By trying to cut in, you are trespassing on the "wrong property." If you persist, you are truly hurting yourself by creating turmoil, turbulence and negative feed to your computer — "Poor me, he loves me but won't leave his wife!"

I have seen many a client fall into a negative cycle or time period simply because he did not pay attention to what was really right for him. Instead of seeking someone who was available, he tied himself down to long months, even years, of waiting around, waiting for someone else's marriage to collapse. Of course, such negative thoughts only boomeranged upon the lonely soul who initiated them — creating havoc and bad times in his life.

Perhaps you would like to attract new and exciting people into your life, but you don't know where to begin.

My suggestion is first, begin with this next exercise. You will be creating an exciting magnetic pull around yourself. Then, unlike the lady that called the TV open-line show, get out of your house at least once!

PULLING THE RIGHT PERSONS TO YOU

Take a position sitting on the floor. Close your eyes, and take several deep breaths in and out to the count of in 1–2–3, out 1–2–3. Tell yourself: "Relax . . . Relax."

Extend your arms outward in the air, to the sides. Command magnetic white energies to be moving through your arms, entering in the hands and moving up the arms, flowing into your body, making you feel alive — magnetic — radiant with positive energies!

Focus on the idea of the right people coming into your life by way of these same magnetic energies that are coming to you.

Mentally say: "I am a magnet for divine good! I now attract the right persons into my life!"

It's downright hard to keep your spirits high when you're down in the dumps with loneliness. There were times in my life, before I met my husband, Terrence, that I felt too tired to hope for anything better.

Perhaps you are trying to keep a positive attitude in the midst of loneliness without the "right one" in your life. If this is the case, you need to give yourself a power boost, like a shot in the arm, to give you extra "oomph" to keep going. Such a power boost also charges your signals with more electricity for the right person somewhere to "pick up on."

Your Quick Power Boost:

1 Find a comfortable sitting position.

2 Close your eyes, envisioning a gigantic white parachute taking you up, up into outer space.

3 Command yourself to focus on *the force of infinite space* reaching you, pumping powerful good energies into your body and your mind. Picture these energies to be the color blue, the vibration of high or divine frequencies. Blue, being a soothing color, also gives a tremendous jolt of healing energy to anyone who dwells on it.

4 Mentally say to yourself: "My energy is positive, powerful, and infinite!" And feel what you are just saying!

5 When you are ready to come back to an external level of mind, mentally count the 1–2–3 method.

By now you will have noticed that in each exercise I have suggested varying means by which you can arrive at your psychic level of mind. This is not a random selection on my part. I have experimented with these exercises for at least eight years and have found that certain approaches to reaching the psychic level work best with certain specific exercises. If, however, you cannot remember how to get to your psychic level with a particular exercise, merely use any method that seems easy and smooth for you. Above all, remember that in merely doing the exercise by whatever method you use in getting to your level, you will be programming your computer radar to switch on the signals. You are arriving at your control tower!

IF YOU ARE MARRIED

You may be wanting to create a more harmonious home life. I see men and women every day who, for one reason or another, have got into a pattern of discord at home. There may be turbulence. Communication may be suffering. The way back to a happy, harmonious marriage is through signaling your marriage partner that "all is well," that home is an oasis for you both. Here is a strong exercise that you can try together or individually:

CREATING HARMONIOUS MARRIAGE

The Steps:

1 Get into a comfortable sitting position and close your eyes.

2 Go into your psychic level of mind as described in Chapter Two.

3 Get into your white overstuffed easy chair and create on your work table the image of a television set.

4 Turn it on with your mind and see you and your spouse on the screen — the picture of love, peace and happiness!

5 Mentally "climb" into that picture and live the feelings of a harmonious marriage for the two of you. (You may find yourself automatically living scenes, comparable to daydreaming. Only this is not daydreaming, it is positive projection of powerful psychic energies.) If you have children, then add them to the picture.

6 When you have had enough, count yourself back using the 1–2–3 method.

As your love and communication grow, the bond of magnetic energy passing between you intensifies. This magnetic energy is a permanent hookup for as long as there is mutual love passing between the two of you.

What can result when one partner is under stress is a shield effect that encircles the one who "is inside himself in worry." This cuts him off from his spouse, who starts to feel cut off. Her computer programs itself with — I'm no good; the marriage is failing! And turbulence around her now cuts her off from him. With both parties cut off, the line of mutual love energy dams up within each. The flow of feeling, communicating and even loving is temporarily disrupted. Can anything be done to end this hideous treadmill effect?

Yes. I have seen many break down the shield effect, both with themselves and with their spouses, by use of their natural mind power.

If you are currently in such a situation you may find that you will have to do this next exercise alone at first, to rebuild that flow of communication.

"My husband doesn't believe in this mind stuff!" retorted a wife of a no-nonsense businessman.

Whether or not he believes is not the issue, I reply. Focus on rebuilding the lines of communication. Worry about the differences of opinion later after you're "flowing."

Your spouse or friend is progressing up the ladder of success, but you are feeling left behind on the bottom rung. This can create a terrible panic, making you feel "no good."

What you have to do here is not let yourself get psyched out. This would only feed your computer with data that says "I am a nobody." And, of course, all systems are go for "poor little you" to be dumped on.

What you want to do on the psychic level is to connect with your mate and send him (or her) signals that you are with him in spirit and emotion and intellect.

How to Keep Pace With a Successful Mate

Since this exercise programs you and your spouse for better communication in general, it can be used by anyone who is feeling that he or she wants to build a better line of communication in the marriage.

In doing the steps that follow, you can create an intensely powerful bond between you and your spouse.

HOW TO CONNECT WITH YOUR MATE

The Steps:

1   Get in a comfortable sitting position and close your eyes.

2   Feel yourself drifting into your psychic level of mind on the count of ten backwards. With each number counted, command yourself to be getting more relaxed and more in touch with your psychic level. (10–9–8 etc.)

3   When you reach the count of one, command yourself to be seated in your inner level at a table with a vase of red flowers on it. You are next to your spouse, and the two of you are holding hands — connecting.

4   Feel yourself "getting" the emotions and thoughts or even problems (if you wish) that your spouse has been experiencing lately: this gives you an accurate picture of what has been going on within him or her that maybe has caused him or her to shut down the lines of communication due to tension.

5   After "listening" and receiving feelings from your spouse, focus

on your telling him that you love him, that you are at his side, that you are on his level of communication. That all is well.

6 Awaken with a count of 1–2–3.

What About The Wayward Spouse?

I have encountered clients who are at their wits' end, trying to keep "the old fires of love burning" while their spouses are looking for adventure.

If in time you find that you are struggling with a fire, or love, that is totally cooled between the two of you, then it is up to your free will to take the appropriate action.

For now you may want to try this exercise to put some "zing" back between you, enhancing the bond that once existed. A reminder: as with all of the psychic exercises, it takes time, practice and patience to create miraculous changes. Keep in mind: these exercises can be done with the magnetism projected from your psychic level of mind.

REKINDLING THE OLD FLAME:

The Steps:

1 Reach your psychic level of mind with the method from Chapter Two.

2 In your easy chair command your mind to see a television set on your work table.

3 Turn it on with your mind and see a favorite scene of your past, involving you and your spouse. Perhaps it was your honeymoon, or a pleasant day that you enjoyed together.

4 Mentally climb into that picture and relive part of the scene, feeling yourself once again connected with your spouse. To further intensify the energies that you are psychically transmitting to him, join hands and feel yourself really hooked up to him.

5 Mentally say to him, seeing him smiling and responding: "We are one. We are love."

6 Count yourself back to conscious level using the 1–2–3 method.

The key for this to work successfully is to mentally release all worry and doubts concerning your spouse once you have done this exercise. If any doubts or depression try to creep in, mentally say: "I let go of all turbulence!"

YOUR PARENTS

Somehow the words "parents" and "in-laws" often strike unrest in the hearts of those who are children. I am not suggesting that everyone has a parental problem, but I do see a lot of people who have unresolved conflicts of some nature with their the parents or with an in-law. I remember meeting with one client who felt as if something were holding him back from living a happy life. Upon tuning into his energies, I mentally saw what resembled a sack of energy attached to the man's back. It, of course, was not a physical thing that I saw, but an image that came to me while in the psychic level of mind. As it had the air of burden, I asked him who it was that was bothering him. "Nobody!" he shot back. "Mother doesn't count — after all she's done to me!" The man was carrying the weight of "mother" on his shoulders. It wasn't his mother who was doing anything to him, in other words she wasn't sending out any energy projection. Such negative projection, as mentioned before, would be an impossible act. What was happening was that the man was carrying, with his *own* doing, the anger and resentment that had piled up on him about his mother. Such a weight had literally kept him bogged down all this time.

I have encountered many persons whose *parents fail to recognize them as grown up. Perhaps you have experienced this.* In such a case you must reach out to your parents through your psychic mind and make the right impression on them — I am an adult! I deserve to be treated with the respect due an adult. In no way are you manipulating them. You are simply laying a new foundation for the relationship.

Communicating With Parents

If you have the luxury of time, then you might want to do this exercise from your deep psychic level, achieved in Chapter Two; however, if the tension is on and you need some quick psychic action, you can focus and transmit just as effectively while your eyes are open.

Envision a white cord wrapped around your waist. This cord

extends from you to your parents, connecting you and them in a cord that resembles an electrical power line through which energies are transmitted. As you have set up such an image, know that such energy transference is now taking place from you to your parents. Also focus on this cord as a power line that is transmitting mutual love as well, so that they not only receive messages of who you are, but they also respond with love and support for your image.

"What if someone is against you?" asked a young woman who was sure that her father-in-law resented the fact that she was a strong career woman.

"You need to do the following," I told her.

In the case of a difficult family member, mentally imagine a white light around each of you. Your arms are outstretched. You are grasping hands. Hear both of you saying in unison: "We are at peace. We are divinely connected!"

This exercise is good for spats, disagreements and general communication breakdowns with parents or in-laws.

You possibly will not be able to change those opinions of your mother-in-law's that are violently opposed to yours. You wouldn't want to, for that would be trespassing on another's private beliefs. However, if she is trying to impose her beliefs upon your life, then she is trespassing and needs to be told psychically by you that her daughter-in-law and son are entitled to a life of their own. The previous exercise is good to establish a flow of love once again. If you need to reinforce that flow with the loving message of "back off and don't thrust your belief systems on us" — then I suggest that you do the following:

Mentally imagine yourself (and spouse, if married) on a mountaintop that is covered with white snow. You are radiant. (If with your spouse, picture the two of you holding hands). See another mountaintop beside you. There stand the parents or in-laws, on an equal-sized peak that is covered in white snow. They are radiant and are smiling at you with love. You are smiling back: "All is well!"

Such an exercise programs your radar to send signals of love to the family, along with the message that you are living your own life and have your own goals (peak = success) to achieve, just as every member of the family does. But you are side by side, in the midst of white snow, a symbol of positive love toward one another.

YOU THE PARENT

Your children have the capacity to be enormously psychic. In my days of teaching high school I encountered many young people who were "plugged in" to the radar signals of others, simply because they had not fully learned to be totally logical. It was fascinating to watch. Even more fascinating was watching preschoolers in a nursery, where they automatically responded to one another, based on the mental signals each was giving out. They had not been told yet about the wonders of the telephone or about certain games one should use to get what one wants from others. Each was automatically acting and reacting from the gut. Each one instinctively knew how to reach the other by the purest means, through that level of the mind that knows no games.

It is very possible to encourage your child to progress with his gut feelings, so that he can better understand and work with them in everyday life. Thus, you are encouraging his psychic mind to develop to its potential. You are not turning him into an illogical misfit, but rather a powerhouse of awareness and stability who would not only better understand people and life in general, but who also would be able to communicate better and in a fuller way!

Communicating With Your Unborn Child

Even the unborn child, being a living consciousness, has a "computer" that can be reached and signaled with positive suggestions for a happy life:

> Both parents place hands over the mother's belly. Together, imagine the child to be healthy, happy and at peace. (Do not program him or her for a set career; that would not work because of unfair manipulation.) Together, say: "Our child (name) is healthy and happy!"

Also, communicating with your child in this way will set up a powerful bond of positive communication that can be with him or her for life.

Communicating With Your Young Child

One of the best psychic messages that you can send to your child is that which uses the power of suggestion through touch.

As you give your child a big hug, say to him or her: "You are such a beautiful person! We love you so much!"

Upon hearing and feeling your energies that he or she is beautiful and loved, your child's computer will condition him or her to be positive, loving, well-adjusted to life in general.

Communicating With Your Teenager

The teenage years can be filled with insecurities and enormous pressures caused by peer groups, school and parents who have the best intentions to communicate but fall short of reaching the teenager because the teenager is walled up in this funnel of distractions.

What can a parent do to break down the wall, to establish open and positive lines of communication and love?

BETTER COMMUNICATION WITH YOUR TEENAGER:

The Steps:

1 In a sitting position, get comfortable and close your eyes.

2 Envision a beautiful white light around you, causing you to relax and drift down an escalator. As you proceed to move downward, command your mind to put you more and more in touch with your psychic level.

3 When you feel ready, envision yourself stepping out onto the lower level, which is your psychic level of mind. You are sitting face to face with your son or daughter. His or her hands are in your hands, resting in your lap.

4 Command yourself to feel an exchange of energies between the two of you. Mentally say: "(Name) and I are connected by the bond of love, which dissolves all barriers."

5 Mentally give thanks that all is well between you and your son or daughter.

6 Use the 1–2–3 method to come back to wide awake level.

I found from teaching teenagers that they eagerly respond to the idea of programming themselves for success.

A Teen's Program for Success

Show your teenaged son or daughter the standard method of reaching the psychic level, as in Chapter Two.

While there, have him envision a television set, and proceed with this exercise:

> See yourself on your television screen as you want to be in the present. Mentally climb into your body and feel and live the experience of you, the success in the present.
>
> Climb outside your television body so that you can switch the channel to your future and the opportunities that it will bring. See yourself. (Don't worry if you can't conjure up an "older" look, the point is that you are in fact creating a successful you in the future, as far as your computer is concerned, and that is what counts.)
>
> Again, climb into your body and live the feelings of you, the success in the future. It may not be clear to you yet what you will be doing, but the important thing is that you are mentally hooking up with powerful success possibilities that await you in the days, weeks, months ahead. Your computer is filing away the data and programming you for success.
>
> When you are ready to come back to conscious level, merely count: "1–2–3. Wide awake. Wide awake."

"What if I want my son to be a doctor and he starts programming himself for success as a circus clown?" asked one frantic lady.

This question perhaps crosses the minds of many a parent, who sees his or her child starting to connect with his own sense of inner power. Many even cringe at the thought of power in the hands of their son or daughter. It is crucial to keep this in mind: When your children come in touch with their sense of power, it is not a power that can cause them to do negative things, or even destructive things. This inner power is a *divine power* that connects them psychically to what is the very best for them, be it people, career or state of mind.

Throughout my teaching years I would give my students some

exercises, similar to those on pages 90-91. What happened, more times than not, was that the student developed a sound self-image of worth, confidence and magnetism. From it all, the student attracted better circumstances into his life. It was exciting and beautiful to watch.

A common question that I get from concerned parents is this: "Can I program my son or daughter to go to college or to pursue a certain career?"

If you *know* that your son or daughter does not want to do what you have in mind, then you are likely to fight a losing battle. Why? Because your son or daughter is already in harmony with another career or plan of action, regardless of whether or not he or she is doing the psychic mind exercises. Remember, we automatically use our psychic energies to *connect* with the targets of our thoughts, round the clock. As your child is connecting with his target, or choice, so is there created an energy bond between that thing and him. And you, in interfering, are perhaps interrupting a divine flow, even though your child's choice may not be the best choice for him. Should you try to manipulate your child, you will experience a backlash of turbulent energies thrown back in your direction, creating havoc in your daily life.

So that your child can get in touch with what is best for him, the exercise on page 91 is a good one for him to try.

If up until now you have been experiencing snags, delays or any kind of turbulence in your personal life, it is never too late to reverse the situation by means of the magnetic powers of your psychic level of mind.

You have *the power* to build a better life for yourself. There is work to do!

6

Improving Your Work Situation

I once asked a crowd: "How many of you work?"

As if in unison, eyes rolled up and mouths stretched to gruesome proportions. They were all making faces at me! ("Are you kidding, lady? If I didn't work, I'd be in the poorhouse!") Work seemed to be a four-letter word, something that you "got through."

In teaching seminars I see many who are in dire need of changing things on the job. However, most seem stuck on a treadmill that they can't escape from. Some reveal that they are too tired to attempt anything new, much less risk that steady income, which they need to support their families.

As one father of five put it: "I want to move up the ladder of success, but that means changing companies and starting from scratch. I would stand to lose ten years' retirement if I did," he said with tired resignation.

Then there was the young woman who complained that she was in favor of looking for a job elsewhere: it was just that her present employer docked her a full day's pay for every afternoon that she spent looking. "I can't afford to look!" she cried.

As I mentally connect with various people and the careers that they are involved with, I see that the majority are held in bondage by their very own energies of struggling and enduring. These are negative signals that broadcast: "I'm not worth your efforts to reward me! I acknowledge and accept my role as less than you!" And the response: the negative aspects of people surface and "hit upon" radar, as iron filings fly toward a magnet.

"But I'm a good person!" cried a male client, who seemed to have talent, brains and personality going for him. What was not going for him, however, was the office staff, who seemed to resent all of his plus factors. Indeed, he *was* a "good" person. "Perhaps too good for your current situation," I said. "You need to get out of there and into something better." Using the exercise on Moving Ahead from this chapter, he "pulled in" a new job with a large company that paid him more, and whose employees related to him much better.

I have seen that it is indeed possible to move through negatives that seem to hold us back. It is indeed possible to succeed despite the "proof" stacked against us.

IT SOUNDS SO PIE-IN-THE-SKY

Such was the statement of a gentleman who attended one seminar. Down on his luck, he had had to borrow the fee to attend. During the seminar he wore an expression of skepticism, confessing to me that he could just not get beyond the worries that were burdening him. He felt trapped. He felt powerless. And the air of negativity that surrounded him encircled him like a wall, preventing him from seeing any farther. For the life of him, he was unable to see better days ahead, despite the fact that he wanted them. Unemployed for eight months, he could not see a job in sight, though he had looked, nor could he see where the next money was coming from. He had a wife and three children to support, and he was scared. He felt sure that life had put him on an endless treadmill from which there was no escape. Months later I was in the same city and noticed that he had booked an appointment.

When he walked through the door to my hotel suite, I couldn't believe that this was the same man. There was something about him that had changed — dramatically. Yes, he was dressed in better clothing. But something instantly told me that he was not the down-and-out "loser" who had attended the seminar several months back. Taking a seat, he began to tell me what had happened to him. I must admit, it sounded a bit "Cinderella-ish." But this man was earnestly sharing the truth.

Admitting that he didn't really give much credence to the thought "You Can Succeed If You Project Success," he nonetheless did some success exercises I had told him about. Putting in a few minutes each morning, he saw himself successfully employed, "though there still wasn't a job in sight," he added. Within three weeks he heard of an opening with a realty firm. "Something made me go to interview for the job," he smiled, adding that he was hired on the spot. In six weeks he sold his first piece of property, a golf course. The profit he made was $350,000. Several weeks after that, he did another deal — this time in New York, making a profit of several million dollars! "Not only did my career life prosper, but my personal life improved as well," he told me. "The money helped, no doubt about it," he added. "But through activating the powers of my own psychic mind, I and my family found an inner peace, because in hooking up to ourselves, we tapped into something much greater than ourselves. This energy united our family in a bond of love that we had not experienced before!"

Today this man continues to be the very picture of success, simply because — as he puts it — "I know the right radar signals to send!"

No matter how dire or muddled the situation, no matter how fixed your own pattern might be, it is possible to change it by putting to use your powerful psychic mind. It could be that you are in a success pattern already. Then, add "more power to you" on the job by activating positive success signals that those around you say yes to.

A WAY OFF THE TREADMILL

If you are seeking a way off the treadmill work situation that you are now in, I suggest that you take a few minutes each day to do some powerful mental work on this, preferably a set time of a few minutes each morning, before you go out into the work day. Keep in mind: *you want to get rid of the entire situation in exchange for a better one to come your way.*

As part of your few minutes' time, do the garbage can exercise (Chapter Three) as a general cleaning exercise. This allows you to dump anxieties, negativities that you feel about facing another day on the treadmill ahead of you. While dumping, envision and command that you are now dumping all negativity related to your job situation. That is all you need to envision — all that you need to do as far as programming your computer *to release* you from negativity that could be holding you back. Your computer will know exactly which material and data to let go of. Rest assured, this is a natural, subconscious process that puts into motion the right energies. You cannot make a mistake.

THE MOVING AHEAD EXERCISE

The Steps:

1 Get comfortable, close your eyes and command that you are surrounded by white light and drifting comfortably down to your psychic level of mind on the count of ten to one. With each count backward, command that you are more and more relaxed. Let yourself go.

2 On the count of one you are in your psychic level of mind — the white room that you have frequented before. To the far side of the room is an elevator. Each time you choose to board it, you can travel to the destination or scene that depicts a goal you would like to see yourself achieving as far as work is concerned. As you journey up in the elevator, think of one goal or job that you would like to see yourself achieving. When it feels right push the button, causing the elevator to stop at the floor that contains the "action" or scene being played of that very goal.

3 Take a moment and think of what goal you want to pursue and achieve. If it helps sit down in the overstuffed white easy chair and relax while formulating in your mind what exactly you want.

4 When ready board the elevator. See the door close and feel yourself rising up the levels of success. When you feel right mentally command that the elevator stop. Note the floor number for your own record (in case you want to return).

5 Step out into the actual scene of you achieving that very goal. There you see the people, the situations and the action that would take place were you to achieve that goal. Take a few moments and live the feelings, the emotions, the thoughts of a person who has succeeded.

6 When ready board the elevator and return to your "special room." Climb into your overstuffed chair and mentally give thanks that it is all happening now for you.

7 When ready count 1–2–3 back to external level.

From time to time on the job you may find yourself feeling certain negative emotions due to the company you are keeping during those eight hours. Think of it — in an office or typical work situation you are literally forced to keep company and communicate with people from all walks of life. Some may be carrying into the work scene negative factors that are automatically intermingling with your own energies. This effect could be causing you to be pulled down or even drained. I am not trying to make you paranoid or afraid to go out into the day. What I am saying is this: the way you feel from time to time during the course of your work day could be due to factors other than yourself. It could have something to do with the energies that others are projecting automatically from their radar bases. I have noticed that the more sensitive a person is, the more he tends to take on the colorations of the people and the environment in which he works.

"Okay! So I'll become hard as tacks, so nothing will get to me!" snapped a teacher who was obviously drained and hassled by the hyperactivity of her pupils.

"Putting on a mask won't change the fact that you are sensitive," I responded.

Many people have this paranoid question: "If I develop my psychic mind won't I become prey to seeing, feeling and knowing everybody's dirty laundry that hangs in the air?"

This I know: the more that you develop your psychic mind potential, using it daily in all departments of your life, the more aware you become of negatives ("dirty laundry" is everywhere) and become positives. You are not prey. You are aware. Yes, you are sensitive, but you are in power and in command of your life because you not only see through the dirty laundry, but you also know what to do about it. Others, who are not tapped into their natural mind power, are fair prey to the forces of negativity thrust upon them as they bumble and stumble about in the darkness. You select your line of focus.

At work, if you feel that the colorations of others are seeping into your own psyche, then take a few moments and mentally declare:

"The white light protects me from all negativity!"

If you feel that you have to deal with specific negative people in your line of work, refer to specific situations outlined in Chapter Four.

During the course of a two-year period of my life when I was bouncing around from one job to another, I found that a good dose of white light in the morning helped to keep me from being drained by the situation that I was about to go into. If I encountered anyone at all during my day, I would mentally envision white light around me, then around him or her — no matter how negative the person. By hitting such people with a white light focus, I was actually creating an air of good feelings within them toward me and the rest of the world. Some, being real stinkers, did not suddenly bow at my feet, but they did back off and not affect me in the least.

Another thing I see that works:

If you have a desk or permanent place that you report to each day, try taking into work a symbol of success in the form of some trinket, decoration, or piece of art — something material, about which you have thought: "Now that's the look of success!" or, "This looks like something that a successful business person would have on his or her desk!" Indulge yourself and buy something that you don't really need, but that looks very much the part of the successful air that you are aiming toward. Take it with you into the work scene. Place it on your desk. And each time that you look at it, train your mind to think: "I am a success!"

I know of a salesman who took this idea one step further and took with him to his office newspaper and magazine pictures of jets, high-powered executives, and limousines — all depicting the kind of business life that he hoped to be leading one day. Of course, you can imagine how the rest of the staff chortled when they saw his "fantasies," as they called them, tacked to the bulletin board. They meant no harm, but they certainly had a good time giving him a bad time! Because he was in touch with his psychic mind, he knew that even though they were harmless, they nonetheless were exposing his mental computer to such literal day-to-day data as "he's weird! — The only house that he can move into is the poorhouse!" Because there were more of them than him, they were likely to hit him with *real negatives* if he told them off. What he did was effective and quick. Each morning before going to work, he mentally envisioned a silly picture of them-in-miniature being tossed into the garbage can. This was by no means a negative force that he was projecting onto them. He was simply programming his powerful psychic computer to reject the negatives that they were innocently dumping upon him. He used this statement as an affirmation: "I release and reject negativity!" Then, for a few minutes' time, he practised the Moving Ahead exercise from this chapter. When they laughed at him at work, he smiled and white-lighted himself again for an energy boost, then did the same for them. After several months' time he had the last laugh; he was suddenly promoted to the position of junior executive, and his job was to travel to foreign countries to inspect the company's branch offices. Need I say? There were limos awaiting his arrival wherever he went.

I firmly see and believe that in order for you to start attracting success in any area of your life, you must start living the part beforehand. Surround yourself with tokens, pictures, thoughts of success in your work situation, and in time you are likely to start seeing physical plane equivalents of those very images that you focused on. It's a fun and exciting thing to try.

Like the salesman in my anecdote you may be surrounded by some type of group force that you have to encounter, get along with and do your job perhaps in spite of. Man is an instinctual animal, so perhaps this tendency to group and cluster in cliques is automatic, universal to any work situation that employs more than two people. Yes, there are at times groups that form for the sole purpose of excluding an outcast, or "meany," in their eyes. There are ways to deal with these. But do remember: more often than not, as you enter most work situations you will find people automatically grouping — just as chickens flock together, just as elephants form a circle around anything or anyone new to them, just as man instinctively builds a fire around his camp site at night. If you find yourself in an employment situation involving office politics and cliques, keep in mind that it may not be as negative as you think. Remember the chickens flocking! Of course, that brings to mind the adage, birds of a feather flock together. So get in touch with your fellow workers mentally through your psychic mind and feel them out. Get a feeling for *why* they are flocking. If, horror of horrors, they were to flock against you, then proceed deliberately with any of the specific exercises from this chapter or Chapter Four to maintain your power over the situation.

SUCCESS WITH PEOPLE

You may find yourself in on-the-spot office situations that require your utmost energy and power in order for you to succeed. What you need is *universal energy* or *divine energy*, that source greater than ourselves that is automatically reached upon plugging into the psychic mind. Since the following situations may require a greater than usual share of psychic energy on the spot, they necessitate your being connected with infinite forces of good. Knowing that such power is behind you, and projecting such power into your work situation, places you in a position of "winning" with others.

Most of these on-the-spot situations require fast action, as you are face to face with a problem or situation that must be handled *now* with the powers of your mind. Before you do the short but powerful exercises below, create a powerful force around you by doing the three preliminary steps. If you should ever find yourself doing the exercises without the preparation steps, know that you can still exert strong influence upon the situation at hand. But be aware that you can be all the more effective by using the three preliminary steps seconds before the exercise — giving you quick, deliberate power.

The Three Preliminary Steps:

1 Take in several deep breaths on the count of "In 1–2–3 ... Out 1–2–3" (creating a passive state of mind enabling you to exert a more powerful psychic influence).

2 Mentally say: "I detach!"

3 Mentally say: "White light" (causing your psychic mind to create a shower of white light all around you, preventing any negativity from affecting you).

Next, proceed with your exercise at hand.

CLIQUES

You are surrounded at work by cliques of people. Worse, you feel as if you don't belong. This tension is affecting your attitude and ability to perform your job well: it is affecting your attitude about yourself. You feel like a failure. What you need to do when confronted by anxiety over this or the actual situation itself is to first detach. This takes away the power that the group force has over your mind. Next, build up a powerful radar signal to them all: I'm divinely beautiful and powerful. This will get the message across that you demand and deserve respect no matter what clique you run with.

You are divinely powerful, a noble being of infinite universal energy who is not to be messed with.

When you encounter a clique, you are quite often encountering a shower of tension that can spread rapidly to your own psychic energy base — giving you a hard time. What you need to do is to protect yourself against such a shower:

> Mentally envision yourself surrounded by a gigantic white umbrella that protects you from the showers of negativity from the clique. Mentally say: "I am protected from all negativity! I am a divine power that nobody can hurt."

Such a simple precaution can save you grief and needless turmoil inflicted upon you by unseen group pressures.

GOSSIP

I remember working in a clerical job once where, to be accepted, I had to take part in the daily gossip — and not just the usual banter about general office news. Outright negative stories were perpetrated to keep alive the image of the poor put-upon office workers versus the cold and cruel management. Whether or not this was a reality was not at stake. What was at stake was each person's mental computer being subjected day after day to the data of "poor me, look how I'm persecuted!" Not only was the morale very low, but I noticed that focusing on such gossip had created an air of defeat around those who took part in it — making it next to impossible for them to achieve any form of success on the job there or to attain any other job elsewhere. It was scary to watch.

You may find that you are surrounded by gossip at your job, or perhaps you know that you are the target of gossip. If so, here is a powerful exercise that you can do to dissipate such negative energies, as well as to stop them from continuing.

First of all, you need to put this whole thing into perspective—small-time people are making small-time noises. Either looking in the group's direction, or envisioning the people in your mind, imagine them to be part of a small-time barnyard scene. If you can, assign a certain animal cartoon style to each "clucking" voice that has been talking against you. See how silly and small-time they look?

Now, imagine yourself standing above them all in infinite outer space. Notice how small this whole thing seems in relation to the billions and billions of galaxies all around you. Spend a few moments taking in the infinite power of good things to come for you.

"I have an associate who never has anything nice to say about anyone," said a woman to my seminar group. "I have to get along with her, but she insists upon putting everybody down. And this brings me down."

How right she was: not only was this woman drained of her vital energy forces, but she was also programmed to "think little," bringing her down to a level of energy where there was less success energy.

Perhaps you encounter people on the job who demand that you take part in their efforts to put down the rest of the world. The gossip at the time may seem innocent enough, but you don't feel the need to be part of this negativity.

Nipping the Gossipmongers in the Bud

Do the following exercise when you are face to face with gossip-mongers:

Mentally white-light yourself, then the other party. Next, envision tall beams of light rising from the tops of both of your heads. (Symbol to computers of divine spirits or "the best" of you both.) Envision the two white shafts arching and "shaking hands," agreeing that "all is well — there is no need to put anyone down."

JEALOUSY

An actress client of mine was forced to work at a Hollywood telephone sales job for several months to catch up on financial debts. She worked in a pool of thirty other women, most of whom resented her being in show biz; they exhibited a vicious "Who does she think she is?" attitude toward her. Many of them had been actresses themselves at one time but had been forced to get into something else, for of one reason or another. Feeling like failures they were only too glad to use my client as a whipping post for their old grudges against those who were pursuing the show-business route. "It was deadly!" remarked my client about the wave of hostility that greeted her each day as she entered the room. She nonetheless survived and kept her own powerful energies in motion, enabling her to land an acting job with a major motion-picture company.

You may find that you are the target of jealousy in your work situation. If this is so, consider this point: if people are actually going out of their way to be threatened by you, and taking the time and energy to dwell upon you, then consider it a tribute to the fact that you have something that they see as valuable and would like for themselves. By having to face you each day and see this "thing of value" in you, it reminds them that you are the one who possesses it, and not they. Their automatic mental response is animalistic by nature. They find themselves automatically lashing out at you, much in the same way that a cougar would do if it encountered a cat from another species. It is a defense for them. The negative part is that such a defense is an automatic attack, directed toward you. You can get "scratched." And worse, your computer can be programmed to make you feel like "something's wrong with me!" How do you fight back without becoming negative yourself?

In the face of jealousy envision yourself to be a walking angel in white, with a shining white halo. As you walk through a room, feel and know that one and all are responding to the angel part of you, or the goodness in you. To all that you meet, envision them to be angels in white like yourself. Feel calmed and elated to know that peace and harmony abound and that your power is a radiant and positive one — attracting to you the angel in all persons.

HOSTILITY

Perhaps you have had to work with people who carry around an air of hostility or signals of "cross me and I'll bite your head off!" Working around such people can be a drain and an emotional strain, to say the least. I get many clients who have to work around prejudiced bosses who maybe "have it in for *all* women," say, or who have a prejudice against a certain race.

I once addressed a group of several thousand men, most of whom carried a macho air toward women. As for their attitude toward a psychic — forget it! — that attribute just made me all the more different in their eyes. Talk about prejudice! Because they felt threatened by any woman assuming a position of power, I was the target of their hostility toward women in general. I had to act fast, let me tell you!

In fighting off the attack of anybody's hostility, you want to make sure that you are detached, you are cool, and that you are at all times in control. All of these points are critical because the hostile people attacking you are psychic, too! If you let them get to you, then you are sending signals to their computers of "I'm your victim that you can take it out on. Hit me!" Now, to turn it all around so that you are no longer a victim of other people's hostility, focus on this thought:

> Those hostile creatures out there are someone else's relatives, in-laws and loved ones. They are someone else's mother, father, sister, brother. White-light yourself and white-light them. Feel and envision all lights connected to each other in one big happy family. Know that you are connected to the "loved one" energy in them, and that they are responding to the "loved one" energy in you. Give thanks that all is well.

I know some people who take this a step further and, according to their own religion, add a prayer for the welfare of the hostile.

"COLORATIONS" OF OTHERS, AND HOW TO AVOID TAKING THEM ON

Maybe you have noticed that sometimes people who work together over a period of time start taking on each other's speaking style, personality traits and even attitudes. All well and good if you want to be that much influenced by the power of others. I am not saying that you can't benefit from the exposure to others. I am saying simply that at times, whether you realize it or not, you may be automatically pulled into another's script, or another's mood, or another's level of energy, and robbed of your own power. When I taught school, I had to take my lunch and coffee breaks at the same times as certain other teachers on the same schedule, all of whom happened to be a group of wise-cracking male coaches who were good-natured, loud and didn't let the presence of "a lady" stand in their way of telling obscene, off-color jokes. They were drinking buddies, and the teachers' lounge acquired the air of a tawdry nightclub. There was no drinking present, of course, but what was present was the coloration of a lively drinking group. Each day upon arriving home, I had to air out by going for a walk to shake loose that feeling that I had spent another day in the barroom. What worked for me, and what I have seen working for others, is this next exercise:

> Before walking into the scene itself, take a moment at home and close your eyes. White-light yourself (as always before an exercise) and envision yourself surrounded by those four white walls of your inner room of the mind. Feel the power, the calm and the confidence you have from these four walls' protection. Give thanks that the power and protection of these walls are with you at all times, protecting you from the coloration of others. If you should be "hit" during the day, mentally call upon that scene of the walls around you.

As you are the one who has to make these exercises work for you in everyday life, it is up to you to select the ones that you will devote time to within whatever daily or weekly schedule you create on your own. I have known some people to combine certain exercises with personal affirmations of their own. If you feel more comfortable in tailoring an exercise, feel free to do so for your own everyday needs. Something to keep in mind, however: in on-the-spot situations it is sudden power that you need, not fancy styling. So keep to the basic exercise as much as possible, even though you may change the wording of your affirmations.

Let's face it — in some way or another, working or having a career means connecting with people. Doing this successfully can only be acheived through the natural powers of your psychic mind.

DOING BUSINESS WITH PEOPLE

SITUATION

Your job requires that you deal successfully with people. You find that their moods, their strategies, and their idiosyncrasies create stress, emotional tension and general hurdles for you to meet each day. Your livelihood depends upon how smooth and effective you are with people. What do you do?

"Shoot 'em!" blurted a lady from the audience one time in response to that question.

Instead, I suggest that you try this next exercise. It can give you "an air of smooth sailing" as you move through your day while dealing with people. A bill collector I knew used the exercise and met with such success in collecting that she started to pass it on to her delinquent clients. Many of them used it to advantage in dealing with *other* bill collectors!

Dealing With Others Successfully

When encountering a person with whom you must get along, "deal" and do business smoothly:

> White-light each of you, then picture a gigantic white sail on your right side that reaches out and surrounds that person's side. Mentally feel the exhilaration and smooth sailing that is now taking place between the two of you (or group of you) as you meet and do business. Focus on the thought that the person is carried along by the smoothness and success of this venture!

I have used this technique in interviews as well as in everyday work matters when I held jobs that demanded that I deal effectively with the public. I know a government clerk who used this technique when once wrongfully taken to court. She came sailing through the proceedings and emerged victorious.

SITUATION

You are meeting with an important person whom you must impress in some way — be it to sell something, to land a job or to convey a certain message. How do you really reach this person, particularly if he or she is a stranger?

I have witnessed men and women being "thrown" in an interview or meeting because of the other person's seemingly impenetrable shell. Had they but known that the powers of their psychic mind could have reached that person and "scored points," I am sure that they would not have been thrown by anything or anyone!

My husband and I have a friend whose manner appears gruff. Anyone who has to do business with him is easily intimidated because of his mean, tough-nut-to-crack exterior. Many people are "thrown" by a face-to-face interview for a job with this man, and the fear that arises from that first impression programs their computers to make them fail with him. ("After all, he's a meany, so why should he hire poor defenseless me?") It's a pity they can't see what a wonderful man he is to work for. But then they had not been informed about doing business ahead of time with their psychic mind power.

You can tune in ahead of your meeting time and actually connect with and get a feel for the person that you will be meeting with, even if you don't know him or her. How is this possible? Remember, you live in a sea of human energies, which abound "in the air." If you were to focus upon a stranger's name given to you, you would be able to connect through the "divine energy wires" to the right "John," even though there might be two hundred men out there walking around with the name of John. This is beyond the scope of one's logical mind, and you could drive yourself silly by trying to figure it out. There have been plenty of documented tests that have proved that one's psychic mind, being a powerful radar, automatically knows which "John" out there you are trying to reach.

In this next exercise you will be "hooking up" with the person that you plan to meet with at some time. Rest assured, your "radar screen" is capable of "picking him up" no matter how little you consciously know about him. When you activate such power from your radar, you automatically signal or call upon the power of something above us all that "knows."

USING YOUR MENTAL TELEPHONE TO CONTACT SOMEONE

The Steps

1 Get comfortable, close your eyes and envision yourself surrounded by a white parachute, free-falling downward on the count of ten to one. With each count downward feel and know that you are getting closer to your psychic level of mind.

2 On the count of one find yourself in your special room of the psychic mind. Climb into your overstuffed white easy chair.

3 See in front of you a telephone console: it is a switchboard of buttons, each representing a person on this planet. Don't worry about which button is linked to which person. (Your computer "knows" which is which). Merely know that you can reach out and connect with anyone at any time. To put yourself in contact with someone, all you need to do is push the button that you feel corresponds with the person you want to reach. (You cannot make a mistake, for your psychic computer is really doing the work

here.) Attached to the console is a television screen that shows you the image or energy of that person as soon as you push the button. (Even if you don't "see" someone or the symbolic picture of energy on the screen, know that your computer is making the connection in reality.)

4 Think of someone whom you need or want to contact — for whatever positive reason — and push the console button. See the screen light up with a picture of that person or with the symbolic picture of energy. *Know that you are now in contact.*

5 Take the next few moments and talk to him in a positive way, either presenting him with positive reasons you are suited for a business deal or job, or saying just "hello," to establish some line of communication. See and feel him nodding yes and smiling back at you.

6 When ready to return to external level, count 1–2–3.

Many a time after "phoning ahead," I have met with an interviewer who stopped in his tracks, remarking: "Haven't we met before?"

"Can anyone pick up his mental phone and call me at any hour?" gasped a concerned woman from the seminar.

"Yes," came my reply, "but keep in mind, that person connecting with you is only able to do so because he or she is doing it with the best of intentions. You don't have to worry about crank callers, obscene callers or even bill collectors!" I chirped.

"I'm on the east coast," she retorted, "so anybody calling me from California better get their time zones right, or I'll hang up on 'em!"

"Yeah," added a man sitting next to her, "I don't like taking calls at all! Don't you have a cosmic answering service that I can hire?"

I think he was kidding. But underneath he was quite serious. Who wants to be disturbed at all hours of the day by energy calls from others? "How does it all work?" ask many.

When you reach out and make a phone call you are not mentally talking with that person as he is in the flesh. What you are connecting with is his psychic energy base that is automatically responding to yours. This is not at all interfering with any thought or any activity that he is participating in as you are doing the exercise. If he is more psychic than some, it is possible that he might feel a wave of something pass through his thoughts. But if he does not know you, this split-second wave will pass from him as quickly as it entered. So rest assured, talking with a person mentally simply means getting a "read-out" from his psychic energy bases. You use the role-playing of talking on the phone because this is programming your own computer to actually *make* the connection. Rest assured also that any such phone calls aimed at you do not in the least interfere with your life, your thoughts as you control them or your emotions. The psychic phone call is but a symbol — a powerful device — that enables you to make a strong, effective connection with the world about you.

SITUATION

You are easily intimidated by others. This causes you to come across as less powerful than you want to appear. How do you overcome this problem? How do you become a powerful presence in today's work scene?

In the face of intimidation:

Look the person who is intimidating you between the eyes, whitelight them and yourself, and focus on the thought that you both are equal in the "eyes" of the higher universal forces that know no discrimination.

I know of people who have done this short, simple exercise in such situations as job interviews, income-tax audits and when in the company of those who tend to rub it in because of their monetary status. I know one woman who used this on a prowler: he looked at her and fled!

I remember a friend once telling me: "If anyone intimidates you, Sandra, just imagine them on the toilet. See how silly they look?"

Great! — It was a strong image, but I noticed that the people whom I was using "the toilet image" on were acting mighty uncomfortable in my presence! Communicating was still a problem until we *both* felt comfortable with each other. So from now on, I resort to my own exercise mentioned above.

WALKING YOUR PATH TO SUCCESS DAILY

I encounter many people who say to me. "If only I had special guidance, I could see my way more clearly!" And I say: "Special guidance is yours through your psychic level of mind."

If you need some special guidance or insight into your career or daily work situation, this next exercise may help. You visualize climbing twenty-one steps, which symbolize to your computer that you are reaching upward for guidance — call it special guidance, personal guidance, divine guidance, you are in charge of what you call it. The point is that it is possible to get tremendously powerful guidance through this technique. The fact that you climb up instead of down happens to work better in this specific exercise than in the others where you drift downward into your psychic space. Going upward has the same strong psychic significance, just as going downward can reach high levels of awareness. So don't let the fact that you go up or down in an exercise throw you. The specific approach that I have chosen is the one that seems to work best for the occasion, that's all. Now to the exercise.

TO OBTAIN SPECIAL GUIDANCE

The Steps:

1 Close your eyes, white-light yourself and see and feel yourself drifting up a staircase of twenty-one steps. With each step that you reach command that you are getting more and more relaxed and in touch with your higher mind or superconsciousness that can give you guidance on any daily matter.

2 When you reach the top, at the count of "twenty-one," see and feel yourself stepping onto a white platform that contains a soft white rug. Take a comfortable position on this rug and find yourself "face to face" with a white energy being that has loving hands extended toward you. This is your higher self that is in tune with the highest and best of directions that you should take with your life. Those of particular religious faiths can even imagine this loving being to represent Buddha, or Mohammed or Jesus Christ . . . creating a symbol to your computer that you are in touch with the very highest of guidance.

3 Take a few moments and, holding hands, ask this positive force questions to which you are seeking answers. After each question wait awhile in the quiet for a reply. It may come in the form of a voice that your inner mind relays, it may be simply a gut hunch that passes over you. Or it may be a swift thought or idea that pops into your mind. Often, nothing much happens in the session

itself. Then, later, during the days and weeks ahead, you start to get automatic feelings and ideas, as if in answer to those questions that you posed. This is another form in which your guidance may arrive. Either way, it is positive and pure guidance that is for your highest and best!

4   When you are ready to return to the external level of consciousness, merely count 1–2–3, repeating: "Wide awake! Wide awake!" a couple of times, knowing that you have been guided by the very best of energies.

"What if I contact a bad spirit from the other side?" asked a squeamish woman.

My answer to her was my basic belief: I do not know exactly where the spirit goes after death, although I get definite sensations that indeed we go on to somewhere. Not having precise answers, and not wanting to play God, I can't give a detailed description as to the "other side" that so many people refer to in relating to life after death. Since my area of expertise is psychic mind power, I can say that when doing an exercise where you are calling upon the highest and best of energies, you are setting the tone, the atmosphere and the results of the situation to be strongly positive, with no negative outside influences. As for using Ouija boards — that *is* playing with forces that are not in the light. Your psychic mind is your best route to "hooking up with" the best guidance possible, be it from your "higher mind," from "God" or from universal energies.

MANAGEMENT, OWNERS AND EMPLOYEES

All of these people have one thing in common — they work. That is why I have thus far lumped them together in the various exercises throughout the book, focusing on emotional and on-the-spot situations that they all encounter in one form or another. Some situations are found more with management than with employees, or more with employees than with management. Therefore, the next exercises will look at specific needs.

MANAGEMENT AND OWNERS

Now that you have arrived at your goals, now that you are achieving the way that you dreamed you would, you want to keep on top. Here is a short exercise to do each morning to enable you to retain the same power that got you where you are today:

> Get comfortable and go to your psychic level of mind by putting a white light around yourself and counting from ten to one.

> Enter your special room and take a seat in your overstuffed white easy chair. On your table in front of you see a picture of a pyramid that is glowing white. See yourself on top of it. Envision yourself to be the picture of success up there.

> Climb into your body up there and live the sensations and emotions and feelings of you — the continual picture of success! Know that your success is infinitely good and positive, and that no one or nothing can take it away from you. Mentally say: "My success, like the pyramid, continues to climb upward!" Know that all is well, so that you can go about your day, assured that you are in continual power and control of your position. And that you continue to attract more and more opportunities for success.

> To return to external conscious level, count 1–2–3.

This exercise is particularly good for one who has achieved a high position, or for one who has come into a powerful role of any kind.

EMPLOYEES

In working for a larger company you feel like a small cog caught in a big wheel. You have ambitions, but it seems as if there are too many obstacles in your way. It's you versus a big system. You wonder if you will ever get anywhere.

To break loose of the situations holding you in place and to start to move forward more rapidly, try this:

> Go to your psychic level of mind by white-lighting yourself and counting from ten to one.

> On the count of one enter your special room and climb into your white overstuffed easy chair. Envision on your work table a picture of you surrounded with white light and that white light lifting you over a series of hurdles that one would see at a track

meet. Mentally say: "I am moving ahead on the job! I am a success!" You can merely view this happening; you do not have to climb inside your body in this exercise.

Next, "clear your table" of this scene and create a scene of something that you would like to see happen to you on your present job — be it a promotion scene, a "raise" scene, or a scene where you are informed that you will be transferred to a better office branch — you pick the situation. Now climb inside your body in this scene and live the emotions and feelings you would have upon encountering such a positive and happy scene.

When you feel that you have had enough, mentally return to your chair and take a few moments in the quiet, commanding that you are now receiving guidance as far as steps to take on the physical plane to make it all happen. (Again, you might get gut feelings now, or perhaps at another time in the days ahead — either way, guidance is coming to you.)

White-light yourself for a boost of energy. Then count yourself back to external level of consciousness with 1–2–3.

If you are satisfied, however, with your employee status and don't have any aspirations of managing or owning your own business, then perhaps the exercise for management and owners might be good for you to try. These exercises are all flexible. And above all, your psychic mind is capable of going to work according to what you personally decide for yourself.

By placing yourself in the middle of the daily work scene, you are placing yourself in the midst of a vast network of radar systems that are not only getting your signals, but are also reacting to you according to your thoughts and what is going on within you.

By learning how to operate your psychic level of mind to your advantage, you will be able to guide, in a positive way, your career and work life. You will be able to move through situations, causing them to work to your positive advantage.

Often, one has to know the future possibilities in business so that one can do a better job of meeting the needs of the market. Or so that one can plan ahead for job projects and family finances. Chapter Ten will show you how you can gain power over the unknown days ahead, enabling you to tune in and "see" what possibilities lie before you.

As for finances, let us proceed to the next chapter. It's time you looked at your money-making potential!

7

Increasing and Improving Your Financial Situation

Let's face it — we live in a world where money talks.

"But I'm a spiritual person!" exclaimed one woman in my seminar group.

She blushed as I eyed her designer dress, her leather shoes and her smart briefcase. I wanted to say, "So where did you get those clothes and accessories?" But I didn't, because she meant no harm, and the harm I would have inflicted by embarrassing her was against my principles. Her blush was sign enough that I had hit home. The fact is that we all, like it·or not, depend upon money to keep us fed, clothed, groomed and generally taken care of. "Money is the source of your life-styles," I said to the group.

"The source of everything is God!" blurted another woman, showing some anger.

I responded: "I personally believe in God, but not as a man in the sky who punishes us with a clap of thunder. I believe that God is energy. Energy, being everywhere, is of divine quality. It not only works through us all, but it works through the plants, trees, animals, birds and material things that make up our life-styles. One of the things that determines what kind of life-style one has is money. It has the power to buy for us nice clothes, homes, luxury vacations and better modes of living. More powerful than money is the all-powerful energy or divine energy that runs through our lives. But on the material plane, we often live our lives in accordance with how much money we bring in. For example, you may want to hop all over the globe, exploring exotic new places. But if your bank balance is only $200, you are limited by the money you have. When you tap into your psychic radar, you tap into greater powers — divine in character — that can rule and affect your flow of anything on the material plane. In order for you to have power over anything on the material plane, you must reach it and affect it first by taking hold of its substance, its energy. The only way possible to affect your flow of money, then, is through your own natural mind powers in motion that can attract money into your life.

"When you stop to think about it, money, like people, is another form of energy. Money has its own electromagnetic aura, which you can reach with your mind signals and 'pull into' your life. The blatant difference between money and a person, let's say, is that the person has his own thoughts, emotions and consciousness, as well as a soul. Money, on the other hand, has none of those. It is paper. It is one-dimensional. It can be affected and lured to your side much easier than a person, who, as you well know, is a complex creature. Money and supply are energies that are all around you for the taking."

"Sounds like you want us to rob a bank!" laughed a retired businessman who wasn't quite sure what he wanted out of my seminar.

I replied: "You live in a sea of electromagnetic energies, all of which are the vehicles by which we can pull in new people, events, and material substance into our lives. By dwelling on thoughts of abundance, though you may have but two cents in the bank, you are hooking up to powerful forces — call them divine if you wish — that can signal to the rest of the world to reward you with supply."

"I need money," confessed the same man, "but I can't pray or wish for myself," he stated proudly, as if waiting for the group to applaud. Instead, they were thinking.

I continued: "I have seen many people who felt it was wrong to pray or to want something for themselves. That is up to them. You practise your natural mind power according to your personal religion and individual belief system. Natural mind power, which belongs to you, is not a patented creation of any single religion or philosophy. It is yours to use in positive ways that you feel comfortable with."

I went on to add the observation that throughout the years I have noticed that the "haves" possess certain obvious traits that the "have-nots" didn't possess. Those who "had" were better fed, better clothed, better taken care of in regard to their health. They exhibited more peace of mind. They also had the vital energy that was needed to live a full, productive life. On the other hand, those who "had not" were constantly weak, poorly fed — even suffering from malnutrition — depressed and too beaten down to do anything but survive. To those who believe in the divine, wouldn't it be absurd to think that man was placed upon this earth to achieve great things while clad in sackcloth, denied food and shelter, waiting out his days until death in ill-health from poverty? I personally believe that we grow from life's struggles and pains. But I also see that a supply of basic needs makes life all the more inspiring to live for.

In my counselings I have seen many men and women who were in a state of poverty. And consequently, many were in a state of frenzy.

"They should have prayed," interrupted a lady in the talk I was giving on "Abundance."

Whether or not they prayed is none of my business. What remained and did not go away was the austere fact that they were without the basic essentials of life, such as food and clothing. How could they have thoughts of beauty and goodness about themselves and the rest of the world? Such dark outlooks made it hard for them to achieve. One such man was living hand-to-mouth on oranges for more than a month. He had come to Los Angeles in hopes of becoming a successful artist. To support his craft, he had to have a job. After many an unsuccessful attempt he was still unable to find a job. His body broken down from malnutrition, and his spirit was on the verge of collapsing. He could not paint without supplies; he could barely get through the next day.

In this case the young artist created his own luck by practising his natural mind power. He soon started to attract the right circumstances and people to him who *did* change things: a man from a noted gallery hired him and also put him under contract to paint pictures as well as designs on expensive clothing, marketed worldwide. As soon as the young artist's "luck" changed, giving him decent essentials for living, his outlook on life improved. With that, his level of energy also improved. Soon he regained his health. And, with so many internal and external improvements, the man was in the position where he could now do his very best artwork. To this day he is still "pulling in" new and positive experiences and situations, because he has tapped into the powers of his natural mind that he was born with. I have seen this artist, and other people like him, take care of their own needs first, and as a result, they were able to take care of the rest of the world through their life work.

You may not be in rags and your life may not be "in the dumps," but in focusing on your material needs, you are acknowledging that you, as a divine being, deserve to make much more of your life through better supply. The only time that you can ever misuse money or supply is if it becomes more important than life itself — if you put it ahead of yourself and your family, perhaps. I have seen wealthy matrons who use it well in creating a beautiful and enriched environment in which to live peaceful lives. I have also seen others who have put more time and energy into gold-plated staircases than into their husbands or children. I feel that as long as you keep in mind that money and supply are important essentials, since you live in a monetary world, you will be just fine, and your supply can grow. But if you place more value on money than on human lives, you will be misusing it. In the spiritual sense of the word you will not be using it in the "divine" way.

WHY THE RICH GET RICHER

Eight years ago, when I became intrigued about "haves" and "have-nots," I began the search for meaning behind it all because of my own predicament. I was recently divorced, living in a strange city. I was penniless, with scarcely enough food to eat. Although I was weak and depressed most of the time, I found that if I used my psychic level of mind to signal to the rest of the world — Sandra deserves better — then I felt better in general, even though there was no proof in sight that anything was *ever* going to happen. I remember lying on my bed (a bare piece of plywood) at night and fighting the dark thoughts of wondering if I was going to live out the rest of my years in such blinding poverty. My thoughts, racing to the week ahead, would try to grip me in a hideous state of panic — You're going to collapse from malnutrition, Sandra! — The landlord is going to kick you out for non-payment of rent, and then where will you go? — Your life is never going to change! — There's nothing to live for! — and on and on into the night, with my turbulent thoughts fighting what positive signals I had sent out earlier.

What worked for me was this next exercise, which started to turn my life around inch by inch.

A WAY OUT OF "THE PITS" AND INTO FINANCIAL SUCCESS

The Steps:

1 Get comfortable, close your eyes and put a white light around yourself.

2 Mentally envision your white light becoming a beautiful white parachute that is now lifting you out of the mire of your present predicament and aloft into outer space, where infinite power and positive forces are yours to tap into.

3 Take a few moments in the quiet of infinite space and focus on the thought that you are a "child of the universe" and that you deserve to be rewarded with positive, abundant energies that are part of the universe. It is your universal right to be provided for and to have supply and to be happy. Let your mind drift to the kind of situation or situations that you would like to have as yours on the physical plane in your daily life — be it more money, all bills paid, lack of financial worry or perhaps big monetary success.

4 Command yourself to drift down into a scene that contains the picture and action of the very situation that you would like to have happen to you. Feel yourself living this scene, with the emotions, the thoughts, the feelings you would feel if this all were happening to you.

5 When finished count back to external level of consciousness with 1–2–3, knowing that you have transcended your present state and have set into motion powerful energies that are making your projected situation possible. As you know, these things don't just happen overnight, so keep at it. It or its equivalent has to obey your signals and come to you.

I strongly believe that in the face of poverty or any form of financial tension, the key to getting out from under it all is to not dwell on your state of unhappiness in that area. Such emotion only puts greater data into your computer, reading: I am destitute forever! Therefore I attract only money problems! By no means should you run away from your problems, but you should not dwell and focus on them either. Focus on abundance instead.

I once worked for a movie producer who carried *focusing* to an extreme — he ignored the debts he was piling up, and put his total attention onto his "Creative Project." My job at the time was to act as a buffer for the irate bill collectors, who hounded the place, while Mr. Hollywood dreamed of making millions. He did not talk "bad times," mainly because he lived in a dream world where they did not exist. Meanwhile, his Girl Friday had nightmares of being swallowed live by stacks of post-production bills. About the time that my own paychecks started to bounce, I decided to move on. Several months afterward I picked up the arts section of the *Times* and saw that this producer had scored a big success with his creative project — a movie that was being marketed worldwide. From time to time I would hear progress reports about how much money he was making — totaling in the millions. Then one day I picked up the newspaper and found an article that told of this producer's legal hassles with investors who were claiming that he ignored their part of the deal. "He is no doubt still in wonderland," I found myself thinking.

The producer was able to "get things going" financially due to his focus. Why things did not go smoothly all along and after he achieved his goal was because his approach was unrealistic and even dangerous. While in the midst of dreaming about making millions, he was running up expenses, resulting in negative repercussions. He could have avoided unneeded turbulence and legal problems by keeping to a realistic budget while dreaming. Granted, there are times when we all have to run up unexpected bills or take financial risks in order to make a venture successful, but in this man's case, his expenses were of a frivolous nature.

You may even now have expenses that are unpaid. At the time, perhaps, they were necessary — they went toward clothing, gadgets, trips or general living expenses. Like the producer you should stay focused on your goals, not letting the bills overwhelm you. Unlike the producer you should be aware of a realistic budget, at least for the time being. That is not to say that you can't splurge once in a while.

I know a woman who, when the going gets tough financially, dresses up the family and herself and treats them all to a nice dinner in a posh restaurant. "Especially when times are hard," she told me, "we all need that extra boost to help us keep positive energy flowing."

And sure enough, something for the better always comes through for her. Unrealistic? No. She is acting with the focus that things may get better. However, if this same woman were to take her family to dinner and pay with a bad check, and do it not only once but night after night, then she — like the producer — would be creating negative turbulence, which would work against her.

If, in the meantime, you have bills that are unpaid, the key is to not let them get to you. Do not panic. Do not be overwhelmed by them. (What can a piece of paper do to you? — is a "game" approach to overcoming an anxiety that grips you.) Here is an effective exercise to do to break the spell of negative energies piling up with bills.

BREAKING THE SPELL OF NEGATIVITY FROM BILLS

The Steps:

1 Get comfortable, close your eyes and white-light yourself. Because bills have taken their time in piling up, you need to take time with this exercise — allowing yourself to drift slowly and deliberately to your psychic level of mind, as described in Chapter Two (falling from pool to pool of colored "water").

2 Once into your psychic level of mind, climb into your white overstuffed easy chair. Mentally envision your bills stacked on your work table. Put a beautiful white light around them to program yourself not to be thrown by any negativity associated with them.

3 Take these "glowing bills" between your two outstretched hands whose palms are facing each other (as if you are holding the stack of bills sideways). Your palms should be about one foot apart as a symbol of "something" that you are taking into your hands — that "something" being the bills.

4 Physically slowly push your palms toward each other so that they meet within a few seconds. Between your palms envision that you have the bills, and that they are diminishing with the power that you are now exerting. Actually get into the emotion of conquering the bills — once and for all! Live the emotions of feeling good about it all. (The more emotion, the more power that you are creating to go to work for you on the energy planes.)

5 When your palms meet, know that you have wiped out all debts,

all bills, all payments that were delinquent. Feel victorious and good about it.

6 Know that you have taken a crucial step toward taking hold of and finally eliminating the bills that you owe!

7 Count back to external conscious level with "1–2–3 Wide awake, Wide awake."

Of course, when you return to the physical level, your bills won't have disappeared. But you will have set up the energy for getting them taken care of in time — and often, soon!

Let's say that you do have some extra money to splurge with in order to give yourself a positive energy boost. Here are some effective ideas that you might try to imprint your computer with: Success is mine! Things are moving!

When depressed, or feeling as if *"Nothing is ever going to happen financially,"* go to a part of town that abounds in nice shops and restaurants. Take a few moments and have coffee or a treat that suits your diet. Reward yourself in the midst of abundance. Spend a few minutes browsing the streets, while focusing on the thought: "Abundance is mine! I am a divine being who deserves the best!"

If you feel in need of a rich atmosphere, go to your nearest museum and browse among the paintings. You may not even be interested in art, but as you stroll through the galleries, focus on the general thought that your life is made richer by the moment! Top off your visit by purchasing a memento that symbolizes success. You can find many choice imports that cost you very little in the museum's gift shop.

If you are feeling under stress about finances, take to a rural scene where you can air out from the pressures of city living. This may be simply a drive or subway jaunt into a quieter, more residential area of town. The point is to get to some place quiet and as pastoral as possible — perhaps to a park, if there is one nearby, that you feel good about. While in that setting take a few moments and sit in the quiet, expressing thoughts that "all is well," "your life is at peace," "better days are here!"

If you are feeling down about your general appearance due to finances limiting your buying basic and luxury beauty items, take time and a few dollars to indulge in something minor yet "nice" for your looks. For the ladies it could be something as simple as a pretty new shade of lipstick or an inexpensive but soothing face lotion that makes you feel pampered. For the men it could be lotion, or perhaps a pair of socks for jogging. Such minor indulging will enhance your computer data with imprints of "I am provided for!"

If any one person or group is hassling you about finances that you owe or are behind on in payments, take a moment and reward yourself with a nice, hot cup of your favorite tea or coffee. The warm sensation will calm your nerves, and the few minutes spent for yourself as a quiet time will be programming your computer that you are in control. Over coffee, let's say, jot down a list of aims and goals that you have in mind related to finances. Some of them may be short-range, while others might be long-range. When I do this exercise, I divide the page into short-range goals and long-range goals. As you list your goals, write each in this fashion: "I give thanks that my bills are now paid!" "I give thanks that my income increases through a job promotion."

Keep your list short and concise. When you have finished making the list, go through each item — one at a time — and command yourself to mentally experience the feelings and emotions you would feel if each were a reality in your life right now. When you finish, mentally give thanks that "all is well" and that "you are now capable of reaching these goals!"

In attracting new things and circumstances into my own life, I have found that once something successful comes my way, it is all the easier to attract more of the same! Or, as the old adage goes, nothing succeeds like success! A favorite story of mine is one by Mark Twain, entitled "The $1,000,000 Bank Note" — where an owner of such a large bank note cannot get it cashed anywhere in his small home town. Meanwhile, word spreads that he is a man of unlimited wealth, and the fact that no one has change for his bank note so that he can buy things doesn't matter one bit. The man's reputation for being a big shot gets him free dinners, free groceries, free everything, with everyone in the town knocking himself out to be in the company of such a wealthy man. Though this story exaggerates the reaction of most people, it still drives home an important point: when you acquire any form of success, you take on an air that makes people sit up and take notice, as if to say — "Hey! He (or she) is worthy of more success!" This ends up with the world "beating a path to your door," as one famous writer put it.

Once you acquire a form of success, you want to make sure that you keep it all moving smoothly in a momentum. This next exercise is good for keeping the success coming in your direction.

DRAWING IN MORE OF THE SAME

The Steps:

1 Get comfortable, close your eyes, and put a white light around yourself for positive energy.

2 Go to your psychic level of mind, using your choice of any technique from this book.

3 When you arrive at your psychic level, take a seat and get comfortable in your white overstuffed easy chair.

4 Notice that the wall that faces you has a window whose drapes are parting, revealing the infinite universe (symbol of infinite positive powers).

5 Notice something else "floating" out there in the infinite universe — a postcard of that situation or thing or amount of money that you wish to keep pulling in. Decide upon one thing, each time you do the exercise, so as to not muddle your focus. (You may not clearly "see" what exactly is on the postcard that is a symbol for what you want to keep pulling in. That is okay, since your computer is, right this second, recording the fact that you are "pulling more successes to you.")

6 See the window open. See and feel a whoosh of blue, positive forces move through the window and into the room, giving you vital, dynamic energy and positive magnetism. Feel the air in the room filled with a beautiful, radiant blue. Contained in this air or force of magnetism are many copies of that postcard coming into the room and dropping into your lap. (As many as you want — the point here being that you are supplied with continued abundance in the "best light!")

7 Mentally say: "There is no end to my abundance!"
"I am a success every day of my life!"

8 Live and feel the good feelings of it all.

9 When you feel ready, count 1–2–3 back to external consciousness.

This exercise can get things moving for you and keep them moving, so that you pull in similar or even better successes from day to day.

"I merely want a raise!" declared one man at a workshop. "I don't want Getty's millions!"

This man, like so many, had a specific financial goal in mind. If you ever find yourself wanting one specific thing or several specifics for your life, here is the exercise for you.

PULLING IN A SPECIFIC FINANCIAL GOAL

The Steps:

1 Get comfortable, putting the white light around you, and go into your psychic level of mind.

2 While in your psychic level climb into your white overstuffed easy chair and command yourself to relax. Place your palms upward, as a symbol of receiving.

3 See in front of you a gigantic movie screen. See yourself up there in a scene where you are in a bank vault that contains billions and billions of dollars — the supply of money in this bank vault is without end. Feel yourself approaching a teller who is surrounded with white light and has wings — a "guardian angel" type figure whose role it is to grant you the money or supply that you need or ask for. The more specific you get, the better programmed you will be for the supply to come your way on the physical plane.

4 Approach the "guardian teller" by saying: "I give thanks that I now have at least (amount) or better, in the best way possible!" (You very well could pull in more, so that is why you program for "at least." And you want it all to come to you in the best way — with no sadness or stress or strings.)

5 See the "guardian teller" smiling back at you, as if to say: "Your wish is granted!" Feel the glow of contentment, peace and general well-being that permeates you as the teller counts the sum into your hands! Live it! Feel your own palms tingle with the sensation of money or supply.

6 When you feel that it is time, give thanks that "all is well," and return to exterior conscious level with the count of 1–2–3.

From time to time I observe people who haven't the foggiest idea of the monetary possibilities that are all around them, with their job or otherwise. If they were to use their psychic level of mind, they could actually get a feel for what possibilities surround them, and are theirs for the pursuing. For example, I recall a woman who was at a crossroads in her career. Having been a professional fashion model for ten years, she was beginning to feel the pressures to get into something creative, where she would not be considered too old. Though she was only in her thirties, her high-fashion modeling career was nearly over because of the younger competition. I showed her this next exercise. She admits that while doing the exercise, "she did not feel much," but in the days that followed, she started getting "gut hunches" to go the route of television performer. Prior to the exercise it had not occurred to her to pursue a career in TV. But, while doing the exercise, her computer put together the data on her abilities and what she could do and combined it with what general area it picked up that was right for those abilities of hers. You might say that your psychic computer is like a matchmaker — it can put you in touch with the energies of those situations and people who are right for you.

If you currently need to match yourself with the possibilities in the world around you, here is the exercise that can place you with the right job that pays the right money, if you choose to make it happen.

PLACING YOURSELF WITH THE RIGHT PAYING JOB OR CAREER FOR YOU

The Steps:

1 Close your eyes, get comfortable and put a white light around yourself. Reach your psychic level of mind by imagining yourself to be at the top of an escalator headed downward. On the count of ten to one command yourself to be drifting downward into your psychic level of mind.

2   On the count of one, when in your psychic level, envision yourself taking your place at a podium, addressing a large group of "white light energy beings" — all of whom represent the talents, abilities, and gifts that you possess in many areas. (This symbol is that of you actually addressing your subconscious.)

3   You begin the speech by thanking them all for coming. You also say to them: "I give thanks that you are now attuned to the right job or career for me!"

4   Mentally envision the white light energies connecting with each other and forming a white funnel that shoots upward, pouring energies through the roof into infinite space (a symbol of reaching upward for guidance).

5   Physically (and focused mentally) place your palms up to receive any guidance. Mentally give thanks that the right guidance is coming through to you. As you envision your palms upward as you stand behind the podium, feel your own physical palms tingling with white light energies pouring into your being, giving you "right action" as far as what direction or steps to take. Ideas, gut hunches, feelings may pop in now — or at another time when you least expect them as you go about your day. Know this, though: you are indeed programming the best of you to be plugged into the right higher energies that are in touch with the right paying position for you.

6   When you feel that you have put in enough time, count yourself back to external consciousness with 1–2–3.

That last exercise can put you in touch with a general gut feeling as far as what opportunities you might pursue — whether you know if there are actual openings available or not. The only reason that this exercise found itself in the "Financial chapter" instead of the "Career chapter" was simply a decision I made to emphasize its ability to connect you-with-your-abilities with the financial possibilities of the physical world, which are all around you. As I mentioned before, so many of these individual exercises can be tailored a bit and switched to do things for you in other categories of your life. That is what is so exciting about your natural mind power — it is flexible.

8

Surviving Losses and Starting Over

A loss of any kind can be unsettling and painful.

"I was hit with blind panic," related one man about his wife's death.

"I was filled with a hideous feeling of being all alone," recounted a woman whose husband died unexpectedly.

"I wanted to end it all!" admitted a housewife whose husband had walked out on their marriage of fifteen years.

I remember a teenage girl — an A student — who was a pupil in my English class. Day by day her grades started to slip to barely passing marks. The reason: her boyfriend had moved away to a college in another state. She was obsessed with thoughts of him dating "all those cute, stylish coeds," as she put it. Because of her apparent loss, I saw this bright, pretty girl slip into the likes of a downcast "reject" whose poise and personality disappeared when her boyfriend left town.

Loss of any kind is something we all go through at one time or another. Few people are ready to handle a loss, particularly one that involves a loved one or friend. Few people have been guided as to what they can do to mentally adjust to severe losses. So most of us blindly go our way, thinking "this won't happen to me." If it does, then suddenly we become a victim to forces apparently beyond our control.

I say apparently, because that is the way it appears — that there is nothing you can do but suffer the loss inflicted upon you. Of course, there is a way out from under the devastating pain and turmoil that you feel from any such loss. There is a way in which to survive loss and to make a new life for yourself.

That "way" is through the awesome powers of your own psychic mind. Not only can you program your computer to take away the hurt, but you can also program your computer to project powerful psychic signals to the world that you deserve to live the rest of your days in happiness, peace and fun-filled times. You can overcome pain, turbulence and sadness with your psychic powers of mind.

WHEN A LOVED ONE DIES

"When Mary died," stated a distraught widower, "I felt alone and as frightened as a child!"

"When George died," relayed one woman, "I was so enraged at him for deserting me and the kids, that I wanted to — kill 'im!" She grinned self-consciously. It was obvious that she would give anything for him to be alive today. But the fact remained: she was alive and had to go on living.

Over the years I have met a large number of people who were faced with the awesome task of surviving the death of a loved one. And in all cases they had to deal with that *air of hysteria* in order to go on with daily living.

I remember getting caught in that air of hysteria myself as a teenager, upon encountering the sudden death of my father. The shock of his death had sent me into a sudden mood of isolation, making me feel as if I were the only kid in school without a father. By day I could scarcely keep my mind on classroom studies. At night was when the nightmares started — grotesque scenes of hearses, the coffin, the smell of flowers. It seemed that I could not get away from DEATH STRIKES FAMILY MEMBER. After several weeks of feeling victimized by this air of hysteria, I instinctively turned to my natural mind power to rid me of the pain, suffering, sadness and nightmarish phantoms.

If ever confronted with the death of a loved one, I suggest that you try this next exercise. If you give it a chance, it can calm the hysteria about death that you may feel. It can deprogram you of negative thoughts and emotions that you can't help but experience in the face of such a tragedy.

GAINING POWER OVER DEATH HYSTERIA

The Steps:

1 For greater impact go to your psychic level of mind using the color technique from Chapter Two. This approach will give you time to relax fully and to allow the powers of suggestion to sink in more than usual. You have been through a heavy crisis; you need to use a heavy-duty approach to reaching your psychic level.

2 While in your psychic level climb into your white overstuffed easy chair. Imagine yourself closing your eyes and drifting, drifting ... drifting off into space in a beautiful white bubble that knows no pain, suffering or panic.

3 While in your beautiful white bubble see yourself being taken to a land composed of your favorite scenery where all is contentment, love and peace. There is no pain, there is no death. All is eternal bliss between loved ones.

4 See and feel yourself visiting and enjoying the company of your lost loved one. If there are fears or sadness that you need to convey to him or her, do so, knowing that you are putting yourself at ease in tapping into the eternal spheres of the collective unconscious where you can tap into the higher or divine energies of anyone — namely your loved one who is no longer on the earth plane. You are not visiting with a ghost, nor are you holding a seance. You are merely reaching out with your mind to the collective source of everyone's minds — and in that source is your own loved one's energy. Energy — being energy — cannot be destroyed. Even though the physical body of your loved one is gone, the energy is not destroyed. Know that you can come at any time to this sphere of eternal bliss and merely be in touch with the eternal energies of your loved one. (How far you take this exercise is up to you — there is no danger in overdoing or in letting your imagination get away from you. In imagining that you are in touch with the eternal

energies of us all, you are programming your computer to no longer be afraid of the hysteria about death.)

5 Mentally say to yourself: "My mind is at peace with the power of eternal love!"

6 When ready return to external consciousness with 1–2–3.

"Do you ever communicate with the dead?" I get asked from time to time. "No," is my reply. "The dead don't talk." If it is communicating with the *spirit* of the dead that the question is referring to — I have my own theories on that. I do feel that we "go on." Exactly *where* we go and what we do is beyond me, and I don't profess to have answers. If it personally makes you feel better to communicate in your own way with your departed loved one, then that is your choice to make. As a psychic I often get deep sensations of other existences beyond our own.

Your decision to communicate with your loved one's spirit is nobody's business but your own. Being a spiritual thing, it is also a *sacred* thing between you and that higher state of consciousness. What I *am* against is this:

I am against people who play at talking with the dead through such devices as Ouija boards, pendulums and amateurish seances — where anybody could fake a "voice" coming through. Steer clear of props and intermediaries who would do the talking for you. You are placing yourself in the hands of people and forces of which we know little. And this is dangerous! It meddles with your emotions and it perhaps calls upon forces beyond the realms of emotional safety — in asking that anyone "come through" to advise you about the spirit world.

I am also against dwelling on the deceased as if they were alive and part of your life's pattern today. Such an attitude can indeed hold you back from progressing into new cycles.

If you feel that you are one of those people who are trying to keep the deceased alive by living in the past, then I would strongly suggest this next exercise. It can help you release yourself from the pattern — without losing any love bond. It can allow you to get on with your life.

LETTING GO OF OLD PATTERNS THAT HOLD YOU BACK

"The Steps":

1 Go to your psychic level of mind through the color technique, to insure a deep and relaxing state of programming.

2 When you have reached your psychic level of mind, find yourself resting comfortably on a white overstuffed couch — alongside the loved one who has passed away.

3 See, feel and experience the peace, calm and happiness radiating between the two of you. Know that "all is well," and that there is nothing to worry about as far as your loved one's well-being is concerned.

4 See and feel the bond of electrical "white" energy flowing between the two of you, showing you and your computer that there is no love lost between the two of you — that the love bond remains the same.

5 See, feel and experience the peace and relief as you envision your loved one getting up and walking to a door that is immersed in white light. See not *that* white light, but see and feel the beautiful white light between the two of you. Keep focusing on: "The eternal bond of love existing between us. We are at peace." (However you want to word it — just focus on this thought.)

6 As your loved one walks through the door into the most beautiful light possible, know that he or she is not going away from you, but rather is in another room or space that is reachable at any time. Know that you are not letting go of consciousness. You are letting go your plight of living in a past where there is no future for you.

7 As your loved one goes into the room, know that your duty is to stay in your own space for now — you have much living to do. Feel your own room fill up with beautiful energies, giving you the urge and drive for living better days ahead.

8 Take a few moments and mentally see and feel a daydream of your living better days ahead — be it traveling, doing something

you have always wanted to do and so on. There is no room for "yes-but" logic here — remember, you are at the controls of your life and are programming for a better life ahead by imprinting your computer.

9 When ready return to exterior conscious level with 1–2–3.

"I have recovered from my husband's death," a young woman told me. "It's his family that won't let me forget! They treat me like a bereaved widow who spends her days suffering." This lady obviously still loved her deceased husband, and whether or not she planned to remarry was up to her; the force that was preventing her from fully living a fresh, new life was her husband's family, who expected the woman to live the part of the sad widow that they had seen at the funeral. She admitted to me that she was still sad about his death, but she was even sadder about the way his family and others had expected her to assume that air of death's victim, when she had released herself of pain and suffering. Her physician, treating her for nervous tension, had claimed that her problem with nerves was really her problem with the in-laws.

Perhaps you have been forced into an unnatural role of suffering victim long after your recovery period. I know of one divorcee whose pain for her deceased daughter was kept alive because Mama — *also a victim, being a widow* — had a common ground on which to relate with her suffering daughter. Both mother and daughter clung to each other — *two lone women face the world!* — and even developed a friendship during the months that followed. Mama even took in her daughter, to live under her roof for as long as she liked. What would have meant lonely evenings for each was now turned into time spent happily reminiscing on times when Papa and the grandchild were alive. When the day came for the young woman to feel the urge to move on to pursue a new life, it was Mama who suddenly came down with mysterious aches and pains, keeping the young woman tied to the home as much as possible.

When faced with the situation of having to shake loose your role of sufferer that others are inflicting upon you, do these steps twice a day — in the morning and at night:

SHAKING LOOSE THE ROLE OF SUFFERER

The Steps:

1 Reach your psychic level of mind using the color approach as outlined in Chapter Two. This will create a deep, relaxed state, allowing you to firmly declare your freedom from suffering.

2 When in your psychic level of mind, take a seat in your white overstuffed easy chair.

3 See an image of yourself and a group of those who tend to keep you suffering beside you on your work table. Notice that you are vibrant, smiling and in good spirits. Notice also that you have a picture in your hands of the "old, suffering" you that your friends or relatives would like to see you as.

4 Mentally crawl into your body up there on the table. Feel yourself holding that sad picture in your hands. Don't spend too much time on it — only enough to make it clear to you that you are looking at a picture that is definitely not you today.

5 Show your friends and relatives this picture, declaring: "I am not the picture of mourning." And with that, tear up the picture, seeing it disappear before everyone's eyes.

6 Now, whip out another picture (from a pocket) and study it, noting that it is the you that you want to be — alive, happy, at peace, excited about new things and people coming into your life. Mentally say to yourself as you study this picture: "I am the picture of health and happiness!"

7 Show this new picture of yourself to the group. See them accepting it with outstretched arms — accepting the picture of the new you.

8 Mentally give thanks that "all is well" with you and with the world around you.

9 When ready, count yourself back to exterior consciousness with 1–2–3.

GIVING SUPPORT

When we encounter the shock of a loved one's death, we need the loving support of those around us — many of whom come to the rescue with flowers, nice cards, foods and visits to the home — turning the home scene into a reunion of sorts. This is good for the bereaved who is distracted by the attention of love and loving hands helping out. What is shocking to the nervous system of the bereaved is that once the funeral is over, the members of the mourning party go back to their homes, resuming normal, healthy lives. It is the bereaved who is left behind, not only by the deceased loved one, but also by the friends and relatives who have done their good deed and are now on to other things. Many have no idea that the bereaved could use some mental support *after* the funeral week, so that he can go on to create a normal and happy existence for himself.

If you currently know of someone who has lost a loved one and is perhaps needing a mental boost from your psychic energies, then by all means try this exercise. It can only send him good energies, enabling him to feel better about the life he must live.

Get comfortable, closing your eyes, and breathing in and out in a rhythmic fashion — inducing that psychic state to be reached at your leisure.

When you feel relaxed, imagine the person who has been suffering to be radiant and at peace, with a smile on his face. See him surrounded in white light — glowing from head to toe.

Mentally say to him: "(Name), I bless you and send you the highest and best of energies!" (Word these affirmations in accordance with your own personal beliefs and feelings, as I mentioned earlier.)

Do not, however, imagine a whole new life for that person. Such "activity" thrown his way on the energy spheres would only create havoc. Merely create peace and good energies by doing the simple visualization. He will feel it.

If you ever find yourself having to adjust to the sudden feeling of being left alone after the funeral, you might try this approach to natural mind power; it will enable you to pick up the pieces of your life and go on.

When hit with that panicky all alone feeling after the funeral, take a few moments and:

Close your eyes, envisioning yourself to be a powerful glowing white magnet, attracting to you the very highest and best of all that life has to offer you. See and feel warm white rays shooting out from the depths of your being, attracting to you nothing but the best of everything. Know in your heart that everything is well and that you are a magnet for new good coming your way.

This exercise has been used by me and scores of others, not only in coping with the "after the funeral blues," but also in coping with moments of receiving bad news of any kind. The force of this exercise will restore your mental equilibrium.

DEALING WITH GUILT

One of the hardest emotions with which to deal on the death of a loved one is guilt. I have met many a person who has exclaimed to me: "If only I had been different . . . perhaps (name) would be alive today!" This brings to mind the day my father died: it was my birthday. I had turned all of thirteen and had made plans, without consulting my parents, to go on a date that evening. (After all, my mental viewmaster had checked the boy inside-out for any character deficiencies and had found him in good standing! Try telling that to my father, who insisted that I was too young to go out with strange boys — viewmaster or not!) My father lost his temper, and yelled "You'll be the death of me yet!" Later that night my father died of a sudden coronary.

To a vulnerable thirteen-year-old on her birthday it was a shock that threw me into an intense state of guilt. (After all, he said I would be the death of him — and here he was, dead!) The emotion and shame of feeling like a bad little girl who had brought on her father's death did not leave me until I started using my psychic computer to reprogram myself. It was then, when getting in touch with the core of my own existence and with the core of the whole situation, that I saw clearly that my dad did not literally mean what he had said to me — that I did not in any way cause his death. Doing the powerful psychic mind exercise that follows relieved me of needless guilt that might have messed up my life for years.

If you find the need to relieve yourself of any guilt feelings — either dumped on you by others or by yourself over a loved one's death — this next exercise can work wonders for you.

The exercise itself will allow you to scan the situation that has made you feel guilty and will enable you to release the burden of guilt in the right way.

GETTING RID OF NEEDLESS GUILT

The Steps:

1   Go into your psychic level of mind using the color technique from Chapter Two — again, using this technique for the most intense approach to a serious matter.

2   Once in your psychic level of mind find yourself seated at a lab table that has a microscope on it.

3   In your mind's eye mentally call upon the situation as well as the people who have been making you feel guilty. As you recall the general feeling of guilt that you have been having — in addition to any people or general situations — see a plain piece of paper forming in your hands, a symbol of you taking the matter into your own hands at this moment.

4   See and feel yourself placing the blank sheet of paper under the microscope, a symbol to your computer that you are now in touch with the factors creating the guilt within. You probably won't see anything appear on that paper, but you aren't really supposed to. What you are supposed to do now is mentally give thanks that you are in touch with the underlying factors of your guilt. You can emphasize this to your mind by mentally feeling yourself looking through the microscope, but as you do remember to focus on your mental thanks, not on trying to see anything that a real microscope would reveal, such as fibers of the paper itself.

5   Relax and spend a few moments in the quiet, accepting the fact that you are in touch with the factors that have created such guilt feelings for you. In this exercise — as in others — do not worry if not much comes through with the first try; perhaps you will start to feel inklings of ideas as the days ahead pass. This happens to many. And this, too, as I have said before, is guidance as well.

6   When you feel satisfied, mentally declare that all is well with you and your life and that proper guidance is yours in the days ahead. Now return to external consciousness with a 1–2–3.

IF YOU ARE LEFT DANGLING

Loss from death or rejection can put you in the role of the one left behind. I encounter many people who come to me, wanting to settle in their minds certain questions that remain unanswered with the departure of the loved one. One widow, whose husband died suddenly while on a business trip, wanted to know if her husband's death was in any way related to the monetary stress that her recent operation had put on their marriage. Another woman, whose husband had left her, wanted to know if there was anybody else, or was it due to something she had done? In any case, the one left behind is the one who sometimes finds himself asking: "Was I at fault? Could I have done anything to help matters?" If you ever find yourself in such a situation, know that you — like others who encounter similar events — are asking a natural question and there is nothing to feel guilty about. You are wondering about the event itself. Perhaps the shock of it — be it death or rejection — has left you asking: "Why?" It is doubtful that anyone can give you answers. Beware of going to a professional who seems to have all the answers neatly wrapped up for you. I am not against getting professional help; it can work wonders. But use your own discretion. In the meantime, if you need to settle that uncomfortable sensation of being dangled from the loss of a loved one, try this next technique. It can alleviate anxieties, and break that tie between you and the destructive, never-ending whirlwind of tension. I have had various people report that after doing this exercise they also received a type of "higher guidance" from hooking up to energies greater than themselves. From such guidance their fears and questions were dealt with.

ENDING THE DANGLING EFFECT

The Steps:

1 Go to your psychic level of mind, using the color process from Chapter Two to achieve a great sense of relaxation and deep programming.

2 Once in your psychic level of mind take a comfortable seat in your white overstuffed easy chair.

3 See and feel yourself facing a "white-lighted being" whose presence makes you aware that you are in touch with your higher

consciousness that is spiritually attuned to what is best for you. It — hooked up with the spiritual forces and energies in us all — has divine knowledge as far as directions or answers that may console or help you.

4 Physically and mentally extend your hands in your lap, palms up — as if to receive knowledge and awareness from this good and divine being, that is actually an extension of yourself — it is that part of you that is your "high self," remember, so you cannot make a mistake or get the wrong guidance.

5 Give thanks or declare that you are now receiving guidance and energies to put an end to the dangling effect that you have felt. Feel the being touching your hands and giving you "right energies" to know and feel what you are seeking to know.

6 Give thanks that all is well and that the dangling is over.

7 Return to external level on the count of 1–2–3.

REJECTION

"What's wrong with me?" you ask in the face of rejection, causing your mind's computer to program you for "wrong" situations of the same nature, if you are not careful. I see men and women all the time who have *felt* rejected by a parental figure at one time — generally dating far back to the days of childhood. Such old data, nonetheless, is strong programming that is still causing that grown man and woman to attract archetypes of their mother or father who they feel rejected them. With such negative data on file within them, they are living their lives based on negative past energies where *something is wrong with them*. The way to overcoming the hold that such data might have on you is to either do the file cabinet exercise in Chapter Three or to do this next exercise, which also takes away the data of old negativity. It also does something else: it gives you a "boost" so that you project powerful signals that you are not a reject to anybody. It can calm you and prevent you from the all-too-prevalent panicking that takes place when one is rejected. If you should ever encounter such a situation, try this.

WHEN FACED WITH REJECTION

The Steps:

1 Go to your psychic level of mind by the color process for deep, effective programming.

2 Once in your psychic level of mind take a comfortable seat in your white overstuffed easy chair. Notice that on your work table in front of you there is a miniature of yourself and a miniature of the person who seemingly has rejected you.

3 Climb into your body up there on the table and "live" the following scenario:

4 White-light the person and then yourself (it doesn't matter who gets white-lighted first).

5 See the two of you boxing — with white gloves on. Nobody gets hurt — you notice. Also notice that you enjoy punching away at the image of this person! (Don't worry, you are not affecting or hurting him in reality. All is in the light and is a symbol for you to be "a winner.") Do this for several seconds.

6 Suddenly the referee declares you to be a winner. (Were he to declare you *the* winner the connotation would be that you wished this person to lose, so declare yourself *a* winner!) Don't worry, if you make a mistake in the wording on any exercise, your all-knowing computer knows the difference. (You can't lose, nor can you make mistakes. So relax and have fun with the exercises.)

7 Take a few moments and glory in this thought over and over: "I am a winner! I am a winner! I am a winner!" — and *feel* that you are! There will be part of you still wanting to cling to the old relationship, but know that whether or not you go back to the relationship, you are setting yourself up for victory, in any which way you proceed. Know that you are projecting strong magnetic energies for your personal successes in the future. The more you get into this exercise, and the more you do it — try twice a day for as long as you like — the more of a winner you can be.

8 Return to external level on the count of 1–2–3.

WHEN THAT FEELING OF LOSS CREEPS UP ON YOU

I have had many a person report that while doing the exercise for loss in the privacy of the home things are fine. "It's just when I'm in public," one lady told me, "I am reminded of how things really are at home!" If you ever find yourself experiencing any kind of anxiety over the loss of a loved one while you are in public, try doing this simple visualization technique that will give you power to move through the moment, enabling you to move on to better and better moments ahead.

In an on-the-spot situation that creates this kind of panic, natural mind power can aid you tremendously. Here is what you do:

Merely envision yourself in that room of your mind you have frequented so often in calling upon your infinite powers of mind. Mentally and quickly recall that one scene on page 132 of this chapter — where you were shown a "door" that connects you with the deceased. (If you have lost someone through rejection, visualize that they, too, are in "another room," mentally within your reach at all times as long as your thoughts are of the highest purposes.) Mentally focus on the fact that no one goes from your life entirely — for your life, being an electrical network of energies, is "tied" to the lives of all beings, with that one "lost" person included. Feel plugged in to him and to the very best of everyone. Know that you are never alone!

STARTING OVER

Once the pieces are shattered — as the saying goes — you have to pick them up and put them back together again. Many people who have been rejected have difficulty in even wanting to go on "because it is all too painful to endure!"

If rejection occurs, you might find yourself asking: "What's next?" You might not care what's next, if you are like some people. But the fact remains — there is something next on the agenda for you in the way of your future and all that it might hold.

"But I can't go on without Tom!" cried one woman whose boyfriend had ended their relationship.

This is a typical reaction I hear from those who are rejected. Another comment that I frequently hear is: "If (name) were a real jerk, I would feel better about him rejecting me. I could shrug my shoulders and say, oh well, he's a bad person — who would want him anyway?" Then the person making this remark goes on to add that the former love partner who rejected him or her was a nice, loving person. And that there must have been something wrong with *him* or *her* if the loved one was a good person.

It is obvious that the person rejected is left dangling and needing reasons for having been cast aside like an old shoe. Should you find yourself needing extra power to enable you to recover from the shock of rejection, here is a potent exercise.

OVERCOMING REJECTION

The Steps:

1 Get comfortable, close your eyes and proceed to your psychic level of mind in this fashion: imagine that you are a bubbly white stream of water that is flowing, flowing, flowing down to meet the ocean, which is cool, clear blue. As you drift along, count from twenty-one backward to one, allowing yourself enough time to drift at your own leisure. Command that you are being cleansed of old worries, old pain, old tired feelings associated with that former relationship.

2 On the count of one feel and experience yourself to be flowing smoothly into a crystal-clear, infinite ocean, whose waters heal you of all wounds, emotional worries and doubts.

3 Feel yourself caught up with a magnificent, white-capped tidal wave, a symbol of powerful energy coming your way. Feel yourself smoothly riding atop it, knowing that you cannot fall off. There is nothing negative about the force of your new well-being, which you accept into your life from this moment on.

4 The wave washes you gently to shore, where you find yourself cleansed, relaxed and feeling a power that can get through anything. Focus on the thought that this same power that is now with you at all times is enabling you to draw into your life better circumstances.

5 Return to external consciousness on the count of 1–2–3.

IF YOU ARE THE ONE WHO IS REJECTING

If you are the one who walks out of a marriage or relationship, for whatever reason, you might have to do this next exercise in order to maintain your own peace of mind and momentum of action in the face of any negative manipulation thrown your way.

Close your eyes and envision yourself white-lighted and walking down a beautiful white road. There are good energies everywhere as you see your path sprinkled with a Disney-movie effect of white sparkly lights glistening on the path in front of you. Know that no one or nothing can keep you from your divine, new good. Feel this and believe it.

MOVING ON TO NEW FRIENDS

From time to time you might find it necessary to move on to new friends and acquaintances. That is not to say that at the first sign of success you tell your old friends to jump off the pier! But at times, when walking your path to success, you may find it difficult to relate your new interests to old friends who either can't relate to the new you or the new interests, or who refuse to do so from their inability to let you change.

You may find that you have outgrown certain people. Family members, because of the love bond, do in time come around in such a case. But in the case of friends who suddenly seem out of tune with the new you, there can be a problem.

I see such situations arising frequently when a person succeeds in some area of work or personal achievement. The newly found success and comfort zone that the person is moving into is not the one he left behind — the one including the friends and relatives who knew him when he was in that old comfort zone. I have also seen in many, many people that those whose friends can adjust to their new successes or comfort zones are the ones who will still be able to be their friends as they progress up the ladder to success. There are others, however, who just can't relate to the new-found success of a friend or family member. Perhaps you have had difficulty growing or accepting someone's climb up the ladder to success. If you have had a problem in this area — feeling as if you are left on the bottom rung of the ladder — I strongly suggest that you do the exercise in Chapter Six (page 96), which will enable you to keep pace with the advancements of friends and loved ones.

If you are the one advancing up the ladder of success and feel the anxieties and even resentment and fear from those who knew you when you were in their comfort zone, then you could benefit from this short exercise. It will send the right signals to one and all that it's okay for you to be a success; that it is not a matter to be worried about.

I once had a friend who, every time I pulled in a success from my writing ventures, got so jealous that we fought like archenemies. When I was down and in the dumps, she would be as sweet as anything — the perfect friend, so it seemed. But let my career advance in any way and I was in for such verbal backlash as: "Well, now that you're a success, you won't need little ol' me!" (A ploy to keep me from advancing by making me feel guilty — after all, look how miserable I was making her feel!) In this case, I had to cut off the friendship entirely, for the "friend" was unwilling to accept my new role of success. The more psychically in tune you get with your mind in general, the better able you are to tell "who is right" and "who is wrong" for the cycle or comfort zone you are in. (As for dealing with family, I have a special section for that one.)

In the meantime, this exercise will enable you to walk your path in the face of the flack you get from insecure friends and acquaintances who would rather see you stay at their level:

> At your leisure, close your eyes, and envision yourself walking down that glorious white path (as you did on page 143, in this chapter). Envision loved ones and friends also surrounded in light and walking their paths, alongside of yours — all heading for the best.

What you have done is to plant the powerful suggestion in your radar — signaling your friends that they, too, can succeed!

DIVORCE AND SEPARATION

Of course, divorce and separation are forms of rejection. So, upon encountering either, you might find it to your benefit to do the previous exercise.

The sheer act of divorce is physical and mechanical in most cases. What is painful and at times even ugly is the time between filing for that divorce and your day in court. That is when I have witnessed many people and their exes-to-be giving each other mental havoc.

Where a bond of energy has existed for so long between a married couple, no matter how close or far apart they are, there remains a channel of energy that still flows between them for a while. I remember counseling a soon-to-be-divorced man who knew that he was doing the right thing. His soon-to-be-ex couldn't have agreed with him more! But then it seemed that he was filled with vague fears and uneasiness about going through the changes associated with beginning a whole new life — after all, he didn't know what lay ahead of him. To ease his mind, I suggested that both he and his spouse do the exercise on page 143. That would be enough to sustain their energies on the right path each had chosen. In the case of couples with children, they should envision their children walking alongside on their own individual paths. As for tuning in to what might lie ahead, I recommend doing some of the exercises in Chapter Ten related to "peeking into the possibilities ahead." When couples part and move more decisively on their individual paths, the old synergy of mutual energies interlacing disperses.

Don't get paranoid — I should add that nobody can break the beautiful synergy that you have going with your loved one but the two of you together.

In ending a relationship or in finding one ended for you, it is always good to "clean your files." I know of one woman who, upon divorcing, went to work on her files by getting rid of anything pertaining to her husband. I know of one man who mentally dumped his wife into his mental garbage can. He laughingly told the seminar that she kept popping out of the can and hitting him with the lid. "What does that mean?" he asked nervously. It was obvious that the man felt uncomfortable in doing the exercise. So his conscious mind was taking the feeling and distorting it, as if to say: "See? You shouldn't do this!" By putting his wife's image in the mental garbage can, it was — as I have stressed before — a mere imprint that he was putting upon his computer, telling it: "I loosen and let go of old energies pertaining to my ex!" He was in no way "doing a bad number" — or even a number at all — on his ex. He was doing the exercise for his own natural mind power.

If you have separated from your spouse and are uncertain as to what the future will bring, this exercise is one that can alleviate anxiety of feeling *I am at the mercy of this situation.* It can create an air of magnetism around you, creating more power for you in your daily life. Whether or not you decide to get back with your spouse is your business. In the meantime, here is something of help.

IF YOU ARE RECENTLY SEPARATED

The Steps:

1 Get comfortable, close your eyes and drift to your psychic level of mind. Envision yourself floating under a beautiful white parachute and floating downward to the count of twenty-one backward.

2 On the count of one command and feel that you are seated comfortably in your white overstuffed easy chair.

3 Imagine and feel that you have a white magnetic band of light around your head, your waist and your feet. Feel these areas to be tingly and magnetic, with gigantic white rays shooting out from you into all directions.

4 Focus on this thought: "I am a magnetic force that pulls to me what is best for me in all areas of my life!

5 Feel the feelings of peace, exhilaration and anticipation as you become aware of your power to attract to you the very best of people and circumstances.

OPTION: If you want to get back with your spouse or love partner, then focus on the same thought as above — with the added statement: "If it is right for me, I now attract (name) back into my life!"

6 Give thanks that things are working for your best interests and for the best of all concerned.

7 Return to external consciousness on the count of 1–2–3.

Keep in mind you are programming yourself for what is right and best for you, so let whatever changes come as well. You are in charge of your life, so take command and accept your power to make things better.

LETTING GO — PARENT-CHILD TUG OF WAR

Quite often I encounter a parent who, upon seeing that his or her child is leaving home, tries to interfere.

I have talked with college students — many of whom claimed

that when they went home for vacation break, their mom and dad failed to recognize that they had grown up. If you are an adult who is still being treated as a child, then it is time to declare your adult-hood through psychic signals.

SENDING THE MESSAGE — I AM AN ADULT

The Steps:

1 Close your eyes and focus on the image of you as an adult.

2 See and experience the feelings of being the kind of adult that you want to be. Feel and see your parents standing in your presence, smiling and reacting positively to your new role of adult.

2 For greater impact feel yourself telling your parents the facts or positive "data" about your being grown up now. See them smiling and nodding in agreement.

3 Conclude this entire "radar session" with the mental affirmation: "Mother and Dad (or however you address them) and I are in tune as adults!"

4 Know that you have reached them with the best of signals — for the betterment of all concerned.

If you are a parent who still has a hard time letting go of the apron strings that hold your child to you, here is a simple but strong exercise that can be done to get the signals across to your son or daughter: "Not to worry! — Mom (or Dad) is okay — she (or he) understands you." Also, this exercise will enhance your own sense of well-being, giving you strength to make the transition.

Of course, you can refer to the exercises from Chapter Five that deal in personal relations, also — but these specialized techniques are good for the specific circumstances on which they focus.

Close your eyes and envision yourself sitting in a circle of family members (if you have but one member in addition to yourself, see yourself facing that member in a friendly pose). See and feel all of you surrounded in a dome of white light, protecting you in a circle of love, trust and inner peace. Know that there is an energy bond that connects you with your family that cannot be broken, pulled away from you or damaged, for it is an energy force that is of the highest and best of natures. Give thanks that you are one.

In the days ahead you will find it easier and easier to let go a bit of the apron strings, because your computer is programmed for you to know that the love is there — always!

COMPLETE COMMUNICATION BREAKDOWNS

I have known some families to get into such fights over parental rights versus kids' rights that the lines of communication break down — with nobody speaking or with a young person moving away from home to escape from the pressure. If you are in such a mess or have the possibility of running into it, I advise that you seek professional help that can aid all of you. There are many fine community counseling services that come to the rescue when a family falls apart.

In the meantime, you do not want to panic over this kind of loss — whether you are the one left at home or the one who is running scared from the home situation. This next exercise may help.

Do the last exercise — only add one thing to it: see and feel all of you joining hands, as a symbol of connecting again. Mentally finish the exercise with an affirmation: "I give thanks that our family is one happy and peaceful unit!"

I know of one distraught man who used this exercise to bring home his runaway son. A woman acquaintance used the exercise to patch up a violent argument that had occurred between herself and her husband versus their daughter. Know that fighting and tensions *can* be patched up — with family members turning to each other for love.

This same exercise can be used to relay the right signals to the family member with whom you have fought — transmitting the message: "It's okay to still love me (us) — let's talk!" Invariably, there might be a phone call or a letter to follow in the days to come. I remember meeting with a distraught mother whose son had packed his bags and disappeared from sight, telling her that he was off to the Amazon, never to be heard from again! Can you imagine how this mother must have felt? There was no way she could write or phone her son. She was stranded and fearful that he was in some kind of danger. I shared with her the previous exercise. It helped to put her mind at rest and into "the hands" of something perhaps greater than herself. The exercise established the psychic signals on her part that she still loved her son, wished him well and gave thanks that he was now in communication with her. Three days later this mother received a phone call from Brazil. Her son claimed that he had had a dream two nights ago where he had seen a vision of his mother praying for his return home. Touched by the beauty of the dream and by the love that came through it, he felt "led" — as he expressed it — to call her. Mother and son talked, and a truce was called on the phone. In a week this young man was back in California and making plans to enter art school — something that he had always wanted to do but had been denied the chance by his mother, who was bent on his becoming a lawyer. Today both mother and son practice psychic exercises — not only to enhance their own relalationship but also to enhance the relationship of the son's new wife with him.

LOSS CREATED BY PHYSICAL DISTANCE

When you love someone and someone loves you, there is no distance between you though you may be separated by physical miles. That energy bond that exists goes right on existing between the two of you, whether your loved one is in Pocatello, New York or Saskatoon. A bond is a bond is a bond. Nothing can change the fact that the two of you are hooked up or connected with each other.

"When my husband is away on business trips I worry that he will meet someone else!" admitted a fearful housewife.

"If that bond is a true one," I responded firmly, "then you have nothing to worry about, for you are bound to each other in divine kinship and love, and nothing or nobody can interfere with that all-powerful energy that transcends man himself."

I knew I sounded like a lecturer, but I see tremendous energy connecting two people who love each other. And if anyone gets it into their head to try to break up such a divine pairing, then they are in for a turbulent time with forces against them. Going against something, such as someone else's marriage, puts one in the position of going against the force of divine good.

In the meantime, it is lonely and painful being away from a loved one, no matter how much you trust one another. This short exercise can help intensify your psychic connection. I have husbands and wives do this while they are physically separated from each other by trips, business and even work situations that take one away from the other for hours on end. This exercise is good to use if you are separated across the miles from friends. It keeps that bond of love active, and you can rest your mind that all is well.

INTENSIFYING THE BOND ACROSS THE MILES

The Steps:

1 Go to your psychic level by using the most intense approach — the colors approach from Chapter Two, thus creating an intense sensation of well-being and power on your part.

2 Once in your psychic level of mind take a comfortable seat in your white overstuffed easy chair. See in front of you a life-sized movie screen. Know that you can use this screen to bring the life-sized projection of your spouse's energies into the room with you at any time. Such "life-sized energies" are like having him or her with you on the physical plane.

3 Create on your screen the image of your spouse or loved one. See him or her happy, at peace and smiling at you through the eyes of love.

4 See your loved one "crawl" out of that screen so that he or she is now totally in your company. Mentally say: "We (or name 'and I') are one this very minute. There is no separation of miles between us."

5 See and feel him or her holding your hand. See him or her listening as you say that you love him or her. See him or her doing the same with you.

6 Focus on the thought that what you have between the two of you is united, eternal and strong. No one or nothing can break you apart.

7 White-light each of you.

8 Return to exterior consciousness, letting your loved one be "seated" deep within your inner mind.

LOSS OF MATERIAL POSSESSIONS

I have met people who have suddenly lost all of their material possessions due to fires, floods or violent storms. Such unexpected losses are, of course, traumatic to those suddenly without. Even robberies — perish the thought — create havoc, with the victim crying out: "Why me?"

Sudden loss, where something that you cherish is taken from you, can almost seem like an act of violence. It can also imprint your computer with messages that you are a victim of unseen forces. Such data you can remove by doing the garbage can exercise or file cabinet exercise. In the meantime, you need to free yourself from the turmoil arising from such a negative event. Here is what I suggest.

OVERCOMING MATERIAL LOSS

The Steps:

1 Get comfortable, close your eyes and white-light yourself.

2 Mentally focus on yourself attracting newer and better material replacements — even though you might have been attached to the old. Take this loss as a sign that perhaps your letting go of the old is now making way for the new.

3 Take a moment, and for every thing lost envision something new and exciting taking its physical place. Don't feel guilty about envisoning a replacement for your great aunt's necklace, for example — only you in your heart know its worth, which money cannot measure. But since it has been removed from your physical plane existence, turn its loss into a "place" awaiting new rewards coming your way.

4 Mentally say: "I am blessed with abundance!" — and feel and live the part of one whose material needs are met and whose losses are replaced with new rewards.

5 Mentally know that "things are well" with you and with the world. Open your eyes on the count of three.

LOSS OF A PET

Loss of a pet? — you ask. There are some who, I am sure, were wondering why I didn't mention *pet* in the sections on loved one. I know many people who consider their pet cat or dog, lizard or bird as a part of the family. My husband and I are among these people. Midnight, our black cat, has not only found a way into our hearts (she's a former street cat turned princess), she has also found her way into our refrigerator, bed, sofa and cabinets. I know that one day she will pass away, and that will be a hard day to face. But I have faced and survived such days before with other beloved pets. Perhaps you have, too. Here is an exercise that can help you, as well as any children in the home who are upset by the loss of your pet.

OVERCOMING THE LOSS OF A PET

The Steps:

1 Get comfortable, close your eyes and white-light yourself.

2 Envision yourself (and family) to be seated with the family pet that is recently deceased. Envision all the family to be in a circle, with the white light surrounding one and all.

3 In the center of that circle is the pet — also covered with a beautiful white light.

4 Envision a door opening up to the pet through which it is scampering with joy. See on the other side of that door a sunny meadow with loving beings taking care of that pet in the best way possible.

5 Give thanks as a group that the family pet is at peace, is looked after, and is in the light.

6 Open your eyes, knowing that everything is fine and that your computer is conditioned to accept the beauty, not the horror, of the passing of the family pet.

Once you learn how to use your psychic mind in the face of loss of any kind, you will be able to see that such loss, no matter how devastating at the time, can be a transition to new cycles of life ahead.

There is a popular saying that goes something like this: "Nature abhors a vacuum," just as a pond has no "holes" in it. If you currently have a vacuum or hole in your life, it is because you are still clinging to that event that created that vacancy. Despite the death or loss of a loved one, you can go on and create a full life for yourself, even if you don't plan to remarry. Remember the water in the pond. Like that water, all of the universe, which is energy, is full of abundance and supply for your life. You merely have to open up to it, and the emptiness or vacuum will be filled.

You have much to live for. Begin right now with your own natural mind power.

You may want to improve your health and energy levels to meet the new responsibilities ahead of you. The next chapter will show you how.

9

Tuning Into Your Body For Better Health

How much effect does your mind have on your body?

Doctors around the world are starting to examine this question. Many are beginning to take a more respectful view of the mind's role in the healing process. One such physician is Dr. Carl Simonton from Texas, who is seeing astounding results in cancer research. Many of his clients are claiming partial to full recovery from using techniques of mental visualization coupled with the proper medical care. Dr. Simonton, like so many others in the medical field, is not only looking toward the twenty-first century as a time for breakthrough in medical technology, but also toward man's awareness of the mind's potential influences over the body. Needless to say, we are living in exciting times — times in which, by learning how to use the powers of our minds coupled with advanced medical treatments, we are getting that much closer to conquering disease and prolonging life.

Dr. Irving Oyle, a physician from California, stresses that we should not view our bodies simply as bodies, but rather as *fields of energy* that can be affected both by medicine and the mind.

Los Angeles physician James Julian is achieving astounding results from his "holistic" or whole approach in treating patients with diabetes, heart problems, cancer and even obesity. It is his philosophy that you are a whole being who needs to be treated in a whole way — with not only the part that ails you taken into account, but also your style of living, your mental moods, your eating habits. It is Dr. Julian's contention that our very thoughts can and do have a direct affect upon the body's neuro-systems, which do, in fact, affect the bodily functions. I had an experience involving Dr. Julian that helped turn my life around.

One summer I was finding myself feeling depressed and down for no reason. On the physical plane everything seemed to be great. I was happy with my life. However I found it difficult to get out of bed in the morning. Into late afternoon I felt as if I were going to faint if I didn't have a candy bar and some soda pop for quick energy. Toward evening I was exhausted "for no reason" again. My husband had gone to Dr. Julian and had achieved incredible results from weight loss, so I ventured in for a checkup. To my shock the check-up not only included a six-hour glucose tolerance test, but also a friendly and thorough interview that probed my emotions and stress levels, as well as my nutritional habits. It was found that my blood sugar was off due to more than one factor. The therapy that followed in the next weeks included a highly unusual approach to an old problem — with the medical staff giving me weekly vitamin-shot therapy, nutrition guidance to follow and advice from the resident cardiologist on how to exercise for my best health potential. Needless to say, with so much emphasis on "improving the whole Sandra," I improved my health in the low blood sugar department and in the whole area of health altogether. It was an exciting and rewarding journey. By the way, I am still on that journey, for Dr. Julian believes — as do many others these days — that excellent health begins with a day-to-day approach, where the patient takes responsibility along with the doctor.

GETTING IN TOUCH WITH YOUR BODY

Your psychic mind can put you in touch with your body, enabling you to project powerful and positive energies on your very body for good general health. This by no means is to say that you should throw away a doctor's care and opt for "just thinking nice thoughts about your ailing spleen!" Rather, I am saying that you have within you the natural mind power to affect for the better the general energies of your body. If you have a specific ailment, seek a physician's care.

And if you are currently under a doctor's care, keep on with it. There is no substitute for the expertise of science. In addition to such expertise you can only aid your body by focusing on and projecting "good thoughts" in its direction. By learning how to project your powerful psychic signals on your body, which is hooked up to your radar anyway, you will be simply enabling yourself to add some good energies to your body. It can only aid your sense of well-being.

GIVING YOURSELF POSITIVE SIGNALS FOR BETTER HEALTH

The Steps

1 Get comfortable, close your eyes and command yourself to slowly drift to your psychic level of mind using the pools of color approach from Chapter Two.

2 When at your psychic level climb into your white overstuffed easy chair and feel it extending at the foot — creating a chaise effect. You are stretched out and oh, so relaxed — tell yourself so.

3 Notice that the room is dark, cool and very peaceful. You haven't a care in the world.

4 Your attention turns to an X-ray screen that is lit up in a soft blue radiance. On this screen is the outline of your body. Command that you see the "energies of perfect health within your body!" (Try to envision soft blue energies — significant of healing and health — moving throughout the body.)

5 Mentally climb into that body form and live the feelings you would feel with totally perfect health. Command yourself to be several things that you pick, such as: well, at peace, rid of pain, and so on. You pick your own feelings and physical states and spend a few moments on each, living them. If you wish, as you experience each trait add an affirmation, such as: "I am well," and so on.

6 When finished find yourself back in your chair, looking now at an entire picture of you — the picture of total health. If you have time, take a few moments and look at details, such as your mouth smiling, the radiant glow of your cheeks.

7 Give thanks (or declare) that all is well. Return to the exterior level of consciousness on the count of three.

Many people come to me complaining that they are lacking in energy. Many have basic goals and plans that they want to achieve, but general lethargy and lack of energy are holding them back. Perhaps you have experienced this yourself. My first suggestion is to get your condition checked out by a doctor, as you should do in all of the situations discussed in this chapter. In addition to what your physician may tell you, this next exercise will improve your energy level in general.

> Get comfortable, close your eyes and envision the following scenario: you are enveloped in a white light, lying on a comfortable bed or chaise. Notice that by your bedside is a glass of water. This is not ordinary water — it is universal energy that you are going to drink to give you more vibrancy, more "life" and more energy in general. As you gaze for a moment into the water, you can actually see an image of "outer space" — infinite power in a glass. Now, feel yourself drinking infinite power from this glass. Command that infinite power to go through every part of you — listing regions, such as, "infinite power is now moving through my head, infinite power now moves through my throat, through my chest, and so on." Command yourself to be wide awake and feeling great.

GETTING IN TOUCH WITH MENTAL STATES

Have you ever found yourself feeling a certain mood and not knowing why you were experiencing it? I remember meeting with a lady client not long ago, who had been experiencing intense moments of fear "for no reason." In tuning into her computer, I sensed that she was physically picking up on some new successes that were coming her way, and she was scared, but in "future time!" Finding out the possible reason behind such fears gave her back her sense of control, and with it her sense of inner calm.

If you find yourself feeling a certain mood or state of emotion and would like to get in touch with it through your psychic mind, here is the perfect exercise to try:

> Get comfortable, close your eyes and white-light yourself. For a

moment think of the mood that has been taking over lately. Then immediately think of a color. The first color that pops into your mind will be your computer's symbol for the mood or problem itself. Next, feel yourself walking through a short oblong tunnel of that color, symbolic to your computer of putting yourself in touch with that mood and the reasons or causes behind it. As you journey through the tunnel, command yourself to experience that mood as much as you can, only this time with awareness of what is causing the mood or problem. (Again — your real awareness of the problem may come later instead of when in the tunnel itself.) When outside, "shower" in more white light, giving thanks that you are in touch with yourself, and release yourself of all problems.

Various psychologists will tell you that it is okay to let yourself feel various moods — there is nothing wrong with feeling blue occasionally or angry or depressed from time to time. But if your feelings seem to be chronic over a period of time, then go to see a professional, such as a licensed hypnotherapist, who can help you even more to get in touch with yourself. There is nothing wrong with admitting that you could use the advice or guidance of a specialist.

From a psychic point of view, I have found this short, easy suggestion to help temporarily "shake" the blues:

When you feel as if you are too down to enjoy the rest of the world, reward yourself with an unexpected matinee; see a movie that appeals to you. Such external reward will feed your computer with data that reads: "I'm in a good cycle!"

When you feel too blue to see people, go by yourself or with a loved one to an amusement park or "fun" place, where "craziness" outweighs the seriousness of the world.

When you feel so down that you want to pull the covers over your head, then do so — but for only an hour or two. Your computer is trying to tell you that you need to be pampered. So follow through with a hot bath, and include with the day's activities a gift for yourself, no matter how minor or silly.

I remember a man who experienced depressed feelings every time he sat down to work. (You're probably thinking: "He and the rest of us!") In this man's case, his all-work-and-no-play regime had created an anger within him that, being inside and unexpressed, had turned into depression. All he needed to lift his depression was some play time. He started taking time to go out to dinner in the evening with his wife, to go away on short one-day visits and overnight trips on the weekends. In no time at all this same man had conquered his depression.

The next time you are hit with lingering moods that won't go away, it would be worth your while to take time to get in touch with those moods. They are trying to tell you something in your psychic level of mind, where all information on you is stored. By reaching that state of mind, you can get a better and broader perspective on not only what is bothering you, but also on who you are as a person. You need not be a victim of your emotions and fears any longer. For any specific fears that you want to work on through your psychic mind, you can refer to Chapter Four (specific negatives) and Chapter Six.

TENSIONS AND STRESS

There are many experts who are beginning to investigate how stress and tension play a part in our health or lack of it. Through my own psychic practice I do see that those people under stress seem to have a more difficult time in keeping up their strength and stamina. For your own well-being and peace of mind you might help fight stress through this next exercise. I have done it before facing a strenuous day, before and after business meetings and after a long week of rushing about. You can do it at your leisure.

TO-THE-RESCUE EXERCISE — COMBATING STRESS

Close your eyes, put a white light over yourself and mentally think for a moment of the stress in general that you have been facing and are about to face. You may not have any specifics in mind, but you are aware that stress has been part of your life and is impending in the hours ahead. After thinking a moment on the idea of stress, envision holding between your hands an oblong stick marked *stress*. Extend your physical hands so that you are living the part of "eliminating stress by your own hands." Mentally and physically push your hands together, eliminating stress inch by inch . . . until it is now gone altogether. Mentally declare: "I am free of stress! All is well! I am in power!"

I have done this exercise on planes, subways, taxis and while waiting to get my income taxes done. This technique also helps reduce head-aches, muscle tension and the four o'clock "droops."

"My only problem," said one man, "is that I can't sleep at night." If you have ever been a victim of insomnia, you will know what this tormented soul was complaining about. Again, if your problem is a chronic one, get a thorough checkup. In my own case, before I found out that my blood sugar was low, I had fits of insomnia for nights on end. And believe me, I would have done practically anything just to experience that safe and comfortable feeling of a natural sleep. What helped me were diet and nutrition therapy, exercise, and this short, effective technique.

COUNT-DOWN TO SLEEP

Close your eyes, and envision yourself surrounded by a beautiful white cloud that is causing you to float and drift — float and drift — float and drift (mentally say this phrase three times, as above) as you hook up with another white cloud that causes you to float and drift — float and drift — float and drift (say three times) until you hook up with another white cloud over you, causing you to float and drift — float and drift — float and drift, as you keep encountering one white cloud after another — floating and drift-ing between each. Just keep repeating this over and over, feeling the emotion of floating and drifting — letting go with not a care in the world — and you will eventually float and drift to sleep.

THE SUBJECT NOT TALKED ABOUT: SURGERY

There is more to surgery than a surgeon merely taking a knife to your body. I have long felt that some people — doctors and lay people alike — view the process rather like taking a knife to a side of beef. I am not against surgery. What I am against is the treatment that one encounters while going through the surgical procedure — with no attention whatsoever given to the natural healing powers of the mind. Yes, surgery is often necessary . . . yes, medication is definitely needed, but some people overlook a very important part of the whole healing process — the person's mental ability to adjust to the surgery and to healing through the powers of his mind.

No one is to blame for such an oversight. After all, if the scientific community that is testing the mind and its capabilities still can't get beyond their circles, squares and triangles in the ESP cards, how can the public be expected to know what the mind is capable of doing?

Author Marilyn Ferguson, in her book *The Aquarian Conspiracy*, attests to the fact that there is a human potential "movement" occurring the world over, in which, among other things, more and more doctors are encouraging their patients to use their mental capacities in the healing processes. As a psychic, I suggest that you consider using the natural powers of your mind in these exercises when encountering the possibility of surgery:

PRE-SURGERY

When you receive news that you have to go through an operation, you might find yourself asking: "Why me?" Perhaps you are one of those people who instantly feel "wobbly knees" at the sight of a hospital. So that you don't have to be the victim of surgery and hospital fears that are unnecessary and negative as far as your computer is concerned, here is an effective visualization you can do to prepare for that hospital visit, as well as for surgery.

> Get comfortable, close your eyes and envision white light around yourself, protecting you from all pain, worries and doubts, about your upcoming hospital visit and surgery. Feel and see this white light around you turning into a strong, positive wind or breeze, as you feel and experience yourself moved in and out of the hospital as if you are caught up in a positive gale. Mentally say: "My hospital (or surgery) stay is a breeze, finding me in excellent shape!"

Remember: the more emotion you put into this, the better!

I know a lady client who, upon finding that she had to go through a hysterectomy, found herself falling into the "old wive's tale" fears of "Will I lose my womanhood? Will my sensuality be taken away with the knife?" In tuning into her I could see that the woman would indeed feel better once she accepted the surgery itself — though I never encouraged or discouraged her to go through with it; that was not my place. What I told her was that I could see that her body would not be "butchered," nor would her femininity or lifestyle change once the surgery occurred. What I also saw, which her surgeon or doctor couldn't see, was that her emotional state after the operation would be down and she would be asking the question: "Did life pass me by?" Had she known the answer to that ahead of time — which she could have through her own psychic state of mind — she would then have been ready and not thrown by any unexpected emotion following surgery.

Perhaps you have experienced surgery, or perhaps — like so many — you may encounter it in the future. If you should, know that your adjustment and recovery can be enhanced all the more oy tne strong, natural powers of your psychic computer whose business it is to program you the way in which you see fit.

POST-SURGICAL PROGRAMMING: FOR BETTER DAYS AHEAD

Get comfortable, close your eyes, and white-light yourself. Envision a loving presence in doctor's garb, encircled in white light also, shining a flashlight of white radiance upon your entire body. Also see and feel the healing warmth of this intense white light go to the direct area of your surgery. Command yourself to "feel the energies of healing" enter your body. Know that such mental programming, along with proper medical care, is now conditioning your body for improved health in the days ahead.

I used this exercise once after a sinus operation, where the effects gave me two black eyes and a nose like a baseball! To the amazement of nurses and hospital staff alike, my swelling and black eyes returned to normal in three days' time.

COSMETIC SURGERY

The term cosmetic surgery sounds more like a visit to the corner beauty salon than to a hospital. And I am sure there are many who visit their cosmetic surgeon as frequently as they can. We think nothing these days of getting a chunk taken off here, a slab added on there, a tuck and a lift and a peel and away you go! — looking younger than ever before. Man is a physical animal and takes pride in keeping the body in shape. But let us not forget the mind's computer, which will be left asking itself: "What the heck's going on here?"

Should you decide upon any form of cosmetic surgery, be sure to have your surgeon prepare you for the mental process that you are likely to encounter as you heal. Noted Los Angeles specialist, Dr. Robert Ruder, is among the new breed of cosmetic surgeons who take just as much time preparing you emotionally as they do changing you physically. Should you undergo any form of plastic surgery, you might consider this technique that has worked for me and for many others. It not only helps you to adjust mentally to the change — even though the change is for the better — it also helps you adapt to the healing process that much sooner.

Adapting to the Changes

Before doing this exercise — where you will be programming yourself for adjustment to a new image — it would be well worth your time to take a moment and decide upon what specifically you want your "new image" to be. And be realistic! A woman I know, whose face was long and overweight, got a nose job from a doctor who was following her instructions. She wanted a nose "just like Marilyn Monroe." Nothing wrong with Marilyn's nose, except that it just did not fit with the woman's individual face. There are many cosmetic surgeons who will not follow unreasonable or unrealistic requests.

Once you decide upon cosmetic surgery with your physician, it is now up to you to take effective steps to adjust to the changes that will take place. In order to adapt as quickly but as smoothly as possible, here is an exercise that you can do three times a day for however long. The New You exercise from Chapter Five is also good, but this one is particularly suited to your surgical changes.

Merely close your eyes, white-light yourself and command to see in front of you a life-sized "mold" of the New You — as you want to look, realistically speaking, of course. See happiness and peace of mind on your face. See beauty. See radiance and white light glowing from your body. Now, climb into the New You and live the part of joyously accepting the New You. If you have time, mentally take the New You into daily situations that you might encounter in the days ahead — and live it all as a success!

SPEAKING OF AGE

Most doctors will tell you that the aging process is a combination of factors — not just the passing of time (and birthdays). In fact, it might be a good idea to check with a holistic doctor or a doctor who is into — excuse me — health, and see what you can do to slow your aging process.

In the meantime, you might want to try this effective exercise.

I have been doing it for more than a year. And when I encounter people who haven't seen me for a while, they remark: "Did you have a face lift? You look younger!"

Get comfortable, close your eyes and put a white light around yourself. Mentally call to mind a time in your life when you felt the most invigorated, alert and healthy. (Or invent one scene that represents this thought — with you being the picture of it all.) Next, mentally "climb into" the you who is youthful, happy, healthy and alive with enthusiasm. Feel yourself putting on a magic cloak that will forever keep that energy a part of you. Know that you are the picture of life and youth.

A friend of ours — a stately gentleman in his seventies — does a variation of this exercise each day, and has no trouble at all keeping up with the younger generation; in fact he out-jogs and outlasts many in work and play.

WOMEN AND MENSTRUATION

Women for centuries have been having to endure "that time of the month" without much mental guidance to make those turbulent times easier.

If you are one such woman who has bad spells during the times of your menstrual cycle, I suggest you try this short visualization exercise.

The thing that you want most from this exercise is relief from tension in general and that oppressive feeling of being down. This particular technique can work, so give it a chance. You have nothing to lose but your menstrual crazies!

Get in a comfortable position, close your eyes and white-light yourself. Mentally envision a soft blue healing light entering the top of your head and moving inch by inch down through every muscle, nerve and organ of your body, giving you instant and intense relief from tensions and pressures associated with the menstrual period. Command that you are "washed" of all problems associated with this. For pain: think of the pain momentarily, then imagine "an energy stick" with "pain" written on it in bold letters of whatever color that pops into your mind. Get rid of the pain in the same process used on page 160 for stress.

ENCOUNTERING THE CHANGE OF LIFE

Change of any kind — speaking from a mental viewpoint — can be an adjustment. Often the particular adjustment of menopause brings with it frustration, emotional turbulence and just plain depression.

I meet many who would not change their age for any other. Yet, when faced with the situation of the change of life, they find themselves going through a sort of shock. It's as if their computer is fed data that read: "I don't know who I am!" And, of course, with such physical hormonal changes, the person involved experiences "highs" and "lows" — creating a conflicting array of computer data, which adds up to disorientation, confusion and even more depression, for it seems that the person is caught up in an unending cycle of turbulence.

I remember an ex-neighbor of mine who in the morning greeted me with a cheerful "Hi! How are you?" By noon, she was quiet and withdrawn when I encountered her at the mailbox. Upon asking her how she was, she snapped at me with a "What does it mean to you?" It was obvious to me that not only were her hormones off, but her computer — being fed conflicting data — was spewing forth conflicting signals. With a physician's help and the help of an expert therapist, the lady was able to regain her sense of equilibrium.

Should you find yourself to be experiencing change of life high-lows, here is a short, helpful exercise that can at least help your mental computer to help you maintain your own balance — either until you get to a doctor or even while you are under a doctor's care. Do not deny yourself the care of an expert physician.

> Close your eyes, white-lighting yourself. Mentally feel yourself seated comfortably in the middle of a white pillow, on a white platform — in the middle of your own inner "white room" — feeling your sense of balance and peace returned to you. Nothing can throw you off of this comfortable position. Feel a coolness (or warmth, if that works better for you) permeate your body as you focus on the thought: "I am balanced and at peace!"

"Hell's bells!" exclaimed a jovial man who had heard about the above exercise, "it works for us males, too!"

By taking an active interest in your total health — by learning how to use your psychic mind along with physician's advice, common sense, exercise and good nutrition — you are on your way to wellness.

10

Preparing For Your Future and Setting Yourself Up For a Better Life

I could hear the store clerk whisper to her customer: "Isn't that the psychic over there?" ("Good heavens — look! She's buying underwear!")

I had to bite my tongue when the customer spun around with a, "Hi — do you have a card? — I need to know if I have a future!"

"Yes — you do," I smiled cryptically. "Don't we all?" Of course, what this lady really wanted was her fortune told, which is not psychic, as I said before. No one had told her that she could see her own future.

Is this possible? — you might ask.

Yes, sweet and simple. What is called your "future" is a collective space of innumerable energies, which have not yet materialized on the physical plane, earth time. These energies, already in existence, are available for you to tap into at any time, no matter if the energies of some possibilities might not physically come your way for years. The time zone that you deal in now is not the time zone of the infinite universe, which contains the myriad possibilities in your future. With the powers of your psychic mind you can learn how to get a general feel for what possibly lies out there for the taking and what possibly could come your way in the days, weeks, months, even years ahead. But remember: the more that you become aware of possibilities, the more you become aware that there are forces that can change things — so it is good to keep a running check on your future and its general possibilities from time to time.

When my husband and I first married, many at his office actually thought that he went home to a wife who "told him his future each evening." Of course, I did take an interest in his future, but not in the way that they thought. Both my husband and I have used this next exercise for our own "feel" of what the future may bring for us. It has helped us "pull in" the right jobs, the right moves to the right cities; it has helped us budget better, and even plan for investments, vacations and day-to-day business meetings. I have even used this exercise in getting a feel for the rush-hour traffic before starting out on the freeway.

Let's say that you want to get a general feel for that business meeting that is scheduled for next Tuesday. Or you would like to have a general idea of the economy — because you want to buy stocks, but you don't want to lose your shirt in the process. All of these things can be gotten in touch with through your own powers of the psychic mind. You may not get specifics as to what color your next car might be, but, and more importantly, you might get a feel for the right time to buy that car, or the right dealer to go to. What I am saying is this — by getting in touch with a general feel for your own future, through this next exercise, you may or may not get certain specifics. But ask yourself — is that so important, when you think that you can at least get an edge on the future and what it can bring for you in general?

You are going to program yourself to "see" a "river," the symbol for your lifeline. Whether or not you get any view of your future possibilities there is not important. Most people find that the mere psychic exposure to such possibilities allows their computer to give them the feeling that they want at a later time. So as you do this exercise, know that you are in touch with your own future possibilities — whether or not it feels like it at the moment. The awareness will come.

STEPS TO GETTING IN TOUCH WITH YOUR FUTURE POSSIBILITIES

The Steps:

1 Mentally feel yourself rising up into space in a beautiful white hot-air balloon . . . feel yourself soaring above the city, above the clouds, above the planets, the galaxies, above the limits of "present time" as we know it on earth.

2 Feel yourself gazing upon a river, which is actually your life in its entirety, with all of the possibilities there, like "streams" and branches pouring into the river.

3 As you glance down at the flow of your life, notice that you are automatically hovering over it — "absorbing" its energies — giving you an awareness of your life and the future possibilities that are flowing at you. (Right now, you may not be conscious of all that is coming — either generally or specifically — but know that you *are* exposing your computer to those realities and it will give the information to you when it is right.)

4 Mentally focus on the thought that you are now in touch with your future possibilities. You now have an awareness of what are the "right moves" for you to make.

5 Feel yourself floating in your hot-air balloon on your way back to the inner room of your mind, where you now spend a few moments in the quiet, further absorbing and getting in touch with the energies you just encountered in your "flow of life." Again, perhaps you will or won't get any awareness right now, but in taking a moment or two in silence to further focus on the fact that you acknowledge such energies, you are priming your computer to give you awareness — if not now, then later.

6 When you feel right, mentally return to exterior consciousness on a count of 1–2–3!

The more you practise the exercise of getting in touch with your own future possibilities, the more in touch you will become with your life and the vast sea of opportunities that are all around you.

"So how do I pull them in?" asked a skeptical man who needed proof.

"Once you pick up on possibilities — good, bad, indifferent," I said, "you then use your natural powers of the mind to focus on the on·s you prefer, giving them reasonable time and energy to your liking; and in time those very things or their equivalents, or *better things*, come along on the physical plane."

The man's look still said: "Prove it!" But this was simply something that he had to try to see for himself.

Once you tune in and get a general feel for your future, you may see some things that you like — and some that you don't like. When encountering the possibilities of things that you either don't want to happen or don't want to be hassled with, there are effective steps that you can take to eliminate those possibilities, if they are not so strong that you simply can't avoid them. Again, I have no answers as to whether or not events and situations are destined. But I do see this — that with enough force and effort on our part, we can, if not avoid a negative event, at least deal with it more effectively by knowing ahead of time of its future possibility.

GETTING RID OF NEGATIVE POSSIBLITIES OR AT LEAST GAINING CONTROL OVER THEM

The Steps:

1 Get comfortable, close your eyes and drift slowly to your psychic level of mind by imagining yourself gliding (with wings) off a tall cliff that overlooks the ocean. As you float downward, count from twenty-one to one, and on the count of one find yourself on a white sandy shore next to a bright blue ocean with whitecaps. This is your psychic level of mind in this exercise. (The ocean signifies "the sea" of possibilities that you are faced with.)

2 On the sandy white shore command yourself to get an accurate picture of that possibility. (Perhaps it has been more fear or imagination than a possible actuality. You want to see — as best you can — that this negative possibility is something that you should be aware of, concerned about, so that you can take precautionary measures.) Sit on the beach, holding out your hands to the water: notice that a dirty bottle washes up on shore and

into your hands. Tell yourself that this dirty bottle is the container of truth, related to that possibility. If you open the bottle and see water, then it is a possibility. If you open the bottle and merely see sand, then know that your idea of "impending disaster" does not "hold water" — a symbol from your subconscious computer that all is well. If all is well, mentally feel yourself hurling the bottle back out to sea, giving thanks that you are free of that possibility. Absorb the positive energy of the sun, giving thanks that you are in the light of new good. Count yourself back to exterior conscious level on the count of three.

3 Should you find water in the bottle, for heaven's sake don't panic! It's only a symbol, not a verdict of doom and disaster. It is simply a possibility that could happen. Now you are advised ahead of time, so that you can work either to stop it or deal with it in the best way possible. Also keep in mind that you are not God, so you do not have all the answers — just guidance from your subconscious computer. Take that guidance and consider yourself one up on the situation, in knowing ahead of time.

4 To program yourself for release and success over the water in the bottle, envelope yourself in white light, then envelope the bottle. Find yourself digging a hole in the white sand in which to bury the bottle, putting it "to rest" permanently. Feel yourself experiencing great joy and peace in doing this act. After burying it, become aware of the fact that this "thing" that you have permanently buried is now returned to dust — it is released permanently from you. (Mentally declare this: "I give thanks that I release and let go of this potential event! It is gone forever!") Also focus on the fact that you are guided to automatically do the right things in the days ahead to further reinforce this fact. Absorb the sun and return to conscious level.

Now to the exciting part — where you can attract and pull in your focus! I know a man who did this next exercise by picturing a certain life-style he preferred. At the time, he was running a car-maintenance shop for another man. Within the course of several years this garage mechanic made enough money from investments on his own that he was able to retire and make a living from his investments alone. Today, ten years later, the man is financially worth a fortune.

I use this exercise to pull in the exact business deals that would be best for me. My husband uses this exercise to pull in the right writing assignments for him.

If you want to start pulling in a better life in general for yourself, here's how to begin.

MAKING POSSIBILITIES A REALITY

The Steps:

1 For deep programming go to your psychic level of mind, using the pools-of-color technique from Chapter Two.

2 While in the psychic level of mind mentally envision yourself viewing a television screen that is "on" with a white light bursting from the screen. Know that this is your life that you are now coming in contact with.

3 As you begin to view each of four channels (each channel is an area of your life) you are programming your life to improve and succeed according to the picture you are creating. First, see the health channel, with a picture of you — the picture of health — as you want to look and want to be. Mentally feel yourself crawling into that picture, and live the part. How would it feel to be that actual picture of health, as you want to be? Be that picture — now!

4 Automatically find yourself seated and watching the next channel — personal life. See yourself (with loved ones, if you wish) — living the life that you wish to experience, either generally or specifically, with a situation or event that you want to experience. Proceed by crawling into the picture and living the part of you who has that scene come true! (If you want several things to happen in your personal life, then live each one separately after you view each one separately on your TV.)

5 Go to *career* and *finance* channels, in the same manner, and apply the same technique.

6 When you have gone through all four channels of your life, sit back and view a white TV screen, giving thanks that your life is a success.

7 Return to exterior conscious level on a count of three.

"I just want to know how to get some general guidance," said one man who was often too tired to operate the gadgetry inside his little room of the mind. (That reminds me of the housewife who took my seminar and who spent her time in her little room refurnishing and polishing the place: "What if someone stops in?" she said seriously.)

You bring into your psychic level of mind the very things that you wish to focus on. If you find that you are too tired to do the exercises according to the precise steps that I have suggested, know that if you do your own general version, within reason, you will be still accomplishing the same thing, but in your own comfortable way. And that's what counts! You must feel good about doing the various exercises from this book. And do not get upset if you cannot remember the precise details. In knowing what you want to accomplish, coupled with a general working idea of what to do, from sheer practice you will be in the position to succeed with these exercises. You cannot lose!

If it is just plain guidance that you want — with no "gimmicks" or gadgetry — try this next exercise. But do keep in mind a critical point: your subconscious computer responds best to the data that is fed through symbolic gadgetry such as used in this book. Colorful, detailed imagery — from such "gimmicks" — is a valuable tool in programming yourself for success!

For an exercise that is quick and less "colorful" — for those who prefer such an approach — here is an exercise that can get you in touch with your natural mind power, just the same. It may not be as intense or as effective as some other exercises in this book, but it achieves its purpose.

GETTING IN TOUCH IN A GENERAL WAY

The Steps:

1 Get comfortable, close your eyes and squeeze your fists, taking in a deep breath. Hold it, and release, letting out the air and feeling yourself more and more relaxed.

2 White-light yourself as you continue to breath rhythmically in −2−3−4− out −2−3−4, and so on. Placing your palms upward in your lap, command that the highest and best of energies are now entering your conscious mind, giving you right direction and guidance for the highest and best of purposes.

3 Spend the next few minutes in the quiet — aware that you are receiving the best of guidance. (You may or may not "get anything" at first, this exercise, like the other guidance exercises, takes practice and "getting a feel for." Also, as in the other guidance exercises, you very well could have the real guidance "hit" you at a later time. But know that what you are doing now is crucial, because you are feeding your computer data that says: "I am in touch with the best guidance for me!" This *has* to cause right direction to come to you.) When finished open your eyes and white-light yourself.

Perhaps you have been through a time with a distinct pattern or "sameness" to it. What causes such patterns or cycles is anyone's theory or guess. Some will tell you it is due to the moon. Others will stress that it is the planets; "Don't you know the planets are retrograde?" they say. And there are those who would argue that we find ourselves in particular cycles or rhythms due to our own biochemical rhythms that affect our outward actions. No one group has been able to supply the answer as to why we have the particular cycles that we do, with each individual in his own cycle, different perhaps from that of his friends, family or neighbors.

I do see this: as we do live in a "sea" of energies, perhaps those very energies — with planetary forces, lunar forces and human thought forces included — are some of the causes of our feeling the way we do from time to time.

Rather than wondering about which one force is the direct cause of your cycles, why not focus on the fact that you are a force yourself, capable of affecting your apparent present-time patterns simply through the powers of your psychic mind.

WHAT CYCLE COULD YOU BE IN?

Should you want to get a general idea as to what pattern or cycle you might be in, and perhaps for how long, you could do this next exercise.

The important thing to remember here is that a cycle is not hocus pocus. Rather, it is simply a recognizable pattern of energy from which you can get a general feel as to how things are generally going for now. To obtain such general guidance:

Go to your psychic level of mind by route of the hot-air balloon method used on page 169, where you got in touch with your future possibilities by viewing the river of your life. Now you want to go to that same river — the flow of things for you — and see it more closely and in a specific way. So, follow the exercise down to and including point three, where you are automatically hovering over the flow of your life.

Now, at this point, give thanks that you are in touch with a general trend (if you wish to name a specific area such as, "general trend for finances," that is okay, too). Feel yourself absorbing the energies from the flow of your life — "present time" — that are now giving you an awareness of what is going on and where you are, as far as a general pattern is concerned.

Float back to your inner room of the mind and spend a few moments in the quiet, receiving and absorbing the general energies of the flow that you were just exposed to. Give thanks that you now have awareness of a general cycle that you might be in. (If you don't get much "help" right now, then know that you will be getting that awareness later.)

Return to exterior conscious level on the count of three.

Such an exercise can give you a helpful and oftentimes specific feeling or idea as to "where you are." Such information can guide you, comfort you and even prepare you for greater successes in the future.

WHAT CHANGES CAN DO TO YOU

One shocking thing I have found is that most people, when they come to see me, have thought that they were in a "bad" cycle, when the reality of the matter was — they were actually in a *transition state* where things were changing in their lives; and their reluctance to flow with the change created inner turbulence that manifested itself in their outer lives as negative events. By getting in touch with their own states of transition — where they could see, in fact, that many changes *were* occurring — they were able to accept what was going on and not resist it.

Of course, there are some who do resist change, even though it is for the better. After all, such change is a disruption of their "safe" life that they had going for them in their last comfort zone, even though that comfort zone was miserable. I remember a woman neighbor of mine many years ago who — every time she was about to get a job promotion — would go through states of depression, skin rashes, binges of overeating and periods of time where she would avoid going into work. Needless to say, this woman sabotaged her own chances to grow and succeed with change. She was holding herself back from the new good that was trying to come to her in the sea of possibilities. Had she consulted a hypnotherapist, she might have been able to deprogram herself of such severe imprintation that caused her to cling to old comfort zones. The last I heard of her, she moved back to her childhood hometown.

I have to fight every once in a while the tendency to hold onto old, safe patterns. At such times I must force myself to realize that I am the one who could be holding *myself* back from important changes. I am the one hanging onto my old comfort zone; nobody is keeping me there. To meet the success that is trying to come my way, I have to move ahead into new comfort zones.

Perhaps success is trying to come your way, too. Perhaps without your realizing it, you have been holding yourself back. Maybe you could be advancing more than you have been in all areas of your life. If you are ready to attract and create changes for the better, then this is the exercise for you. Try it at least twice a day.

ATTRACTING CHANGES FOR THE BETTER

The Steps:

1 Get comfortable, close your eyes and mentally put a white light around yourself. Command that you are gently sliding into your psychic level of mind.

2 See and feel yourself in your own little room.

3 See and feel the window to the universe opening, revealing infinite good out there, all around you twenty-four hours a day.

4 Feel and experience a strong, positive gust of "universal energy" sweeping into the room, bringing with it changes for the better. (The gust of "wind" is bright blue, signifying energies of the highest and most positive nature.)

5 You may or may not picture actual events and specifics — this is up to you. You can get as specific with all of these exercises as you wish. But know that you are attracting to you the very best of changes for the better.

6 Mentally live the part of experiencing changes for the better, and feel yourself adapting to them easily. If you have family members, see and feel them in the room with you adapting right along with you, making it a smooth time of transition for *all* concerned.

7 Mentally give thanks that all is moving along in the best way possible. Return to exterior level on the count of three.

The next time you start wondering about what the future will bring, know that the future possibilities exist now on both the energy planes and material planes. And that it is possible to tap into your future possibilities and make them eventually a functional part of your life. You possess a remarkable gift that can enable you to connect with people, with the world around you, with yourself — and your own future potential and possibilities.

Your future is out there, now. And it begins with you! You can make it all "happen" through your own natural mind power.

Author's Note

The next time you see a "performing psychic" on television, remember: he or she is not a performing seal. That person is no better nor any different than you with respect to his or her natural mind powers. If he or she chooses to awe the audience with various experiences of tracking down missing bodies, that is that particular person's focus. You have a focus to pursue that can awe yourself, your family and friends:

You can literally improve and change the quality of your own life through your own super natural mind.

You are that special.

Index